AF661344

SCHOLASTIC

Book of BOONS & CURSES in Hindu Mythology

SUNITA PANT BANSAL

Illustrated by
Boski Jain

To all those who pick up this book,
thank you for giving my words a chance.

Text © 2024 Sunita Pant Bansal
Illustrations © 2024 Scholastic India Pvt. Ltd.

All rights reserved.

Published by Scholastic India Pvt. Ltd.
A subsidiary of Scholastic Inc., New York, 10012 (USA).
Publishers since 1920, with international operations in Canada, Australia, New Zealand, the United Kingdom, India, and Hong Kong.

No part of this publication may be reproduced in whole or in part, or stored in a retrieval system, or transmitted in any form or by any means, electronic, mechanical, photocopying, recording, or otherwise without the written permission of the publisher.

For information regarding permission, write to:
Scholastic India Pvt. Ltd.
A-27, Ground Floor, Sigma Centre
Infocity-1, Sector 34, Gurgaon-122001 (India)

First edition: December 2024

ISBN-13: 978-93-5954-231-7

Printed in India at Polykam offset New Delhi 110028

Contents

Introduction

Mythological stories get created because we want to know the reason for everything that happens in our lives. Hindu mythology explains the reasons using the philosophy of Karma, which says that our own actions determine our future. Hence, we are the cause of all that is happening to us!

This collection of mythological stories helps us understand the philosophy of Karma and shows how boons and curses give direction to a person's life. And, how we can change that direction if we want to.

Boons and curses are an important part of any mythology – be it Greek, Roman, Celtic, or Hindu. The difference is that in other cultures, boons and curses come only from God, whereas in Hindu mythology, anyone can curse anyone. Even the gods are not spared from being cursed!

It's not necessary for a curse to be a bad thing and a boon to be a good thing. They can be interchangeable, depending on how a person makes use of them.

Shravana Kumar's parents' curse on an heirless Dasharatha made him realize that he had to have sons to suffer separation. It gave him hope to conduct a fire-sacrifice by which he was blessed with four sons or heirs. And hence, Dasharatha turned his curse to a boon.

At the same time, Dasharatha's boon to his wife Kaikeyi led his son

Rama to exile. This, to Dasharatha, seemed like a curse leading to his own death. On the other hand, Rama's exile resulted in his destroying all the demons including Ravana, ridding the earth of evil, which was a boon for the people.

In mythological stories, demons are seen praying for immortality, as they do not want to die! This is obviously not possible, because whoever is born must die. So, the demons are given the choice to pick the method of their death. Tarakasura, Tripurasura, and Ravana set the most bizarre, the toughest of conditions for their death, but finally their karma takes over to destroy them.

Whether gods or demons, everyone faces the consequences of their own actions. Monkey king Vali was killed by Rama who was hidden behind the bushes. Rama was aware of his wrongdoing, though it was needed to be done at that time. So, he blessed Vali to kill him in his Krishna incarnation in the same manner. Consequently, Vali was born as Jara the hunter and killed Krishna with his arrow, shooting from behind the bushes.

Everything in the Hindu world is reborn. Boons and curses are a way to show that whatever we do comes back to us. Clearly, what we make of our future is in our hands!

Tarakasura's Boon, Birth of Kartikeya

Demon Vajranga was born to sage Kashyapa and his wife Diti. He was a powerful demon, born to conquer the gods. And he did just that. However, he was unhappy with his own demonic nature.

Once, Vajranga captured the gods along with their king, Indra, and punished them on his mother's orders. Indra was Kashyapa's other wife Aditi's son, hence, Vajranga's half-brother. Aditi complained to Brahma.

Vajranga promptly released everyone on Brahma's request, stating that he had done what his mother had asked him to. He had no personal grudge against the demons...at least not till that time. Pleased with his actions and words, Brahma created a beautiful and loving wife for Vajranga, called Varangi.

Vajranga lived a happy and peaceful life in a forest with Varangi. But little did they know what was in store for them!

One day, Vajranga decided to do penance to get rid of his demonic nature. It was a long and arduous penance. A long penance in those times went on for many years, and was done in a secluded place, far away from home.

Varangi was living alone in their hut.

DID YOU KNOW?

During **penance** a person meditates on the god being prayed to, chanting mantras in praise of that god. The penance ends when the god appears in person and grants a boon.

One morning, she was tending to her plants as usual, when she heard strange loud sounds from behind her hut.

'WHOOOOSHHH! SWISHHH! CRRRRACKKK!'

'Sounds like a storm hitting the trees, but there is no wind!' Confused, Varangi went to check the forest behind her hut.

To her shock, she saw a huge monkey leaping about from tree to tree, breaking branches, pulling vines, and destroying the trees.

'Why are you wrecking the trees that give you shelter and food?' asked Varangi.

In response, the monkey destroyed some more trees, sniggered at Varangi, and leapt off. The demoness was relieved that the destruction was over.

But it was just the beginning!

Varangi picked up the broken branches of the trees and put them on one side of her hut. 'I can use them to light fire,' she said to herself.

She went back to continue tending to her plants. To her utter dismay, she discovered that the grassy patch in front of her hut was no more! The plants she loved so much, lay strewn – their tender flowers and leaves all withered and dead.

With tears blinding her eyes, Varangi looked around for the culprit. And what did she see?

A plump innocent-looking sheep was merrily grazing the leftover plants!

'What have you done, you silly sheep!' The demoness felt helpless as the sheep looked at her with startled eyes, bleated, and trotted away into the forest.

Sure, there were monkeys in the forest, but where did this sheep come from?

Varangi went back into her hut, feeling miserable, when she noticed a snake! It was about to attack when she picked up a vessel and threw at it. She was full of anger with what was happening around her and was in no mood to spare the snake. But it swiftly slithered away into the forest.

Who was behind all this?

Indra, the king of gods! He loved to play pranks on unsuspecting people, gods, or demons. This was his idea of entertainment.

When Vajranga returned home and saw all the mess, he could tell who was behind this ruckus at once. He immediately decided to do penance once again to find a remedy for Indra's unjust behaviour.

Brahma was already happy with the demon's devotion, so he readily appeared.

'Why do you want to do penance again? Tell me what you desire. You have never asked for a boon, now is the time to do so.'

'O Lord, I did penance for so many years to get rid of my demonic nature. I've never had any grudge against my half-brother or any other god. But Indra's misbehaviour towards my wife in my absence is unacceptable to me...hence this penance!' Vajranga was visibly upset.

'If you want to bless me then give me a powerful son, who will defeat Indra and teach him a lesson. We demons are tired of Indra and his friends troubling us all the time,' he added.

'So be it!' With Brahma's blessing, soon Varangi gave birth to a son named Tarakasura.

Tarakasura grew up to be a mighty demon. But he knew that to fight Indra and the other gods, he needed to become more powerful than anyone in the world. He also decided to pray to Brahma, the god known for his generosity in giving boons.

'You are already very powerful, what else do you want?' Brahma asked.

Tarakasura had two demands, 'I want to be the most powerful person in the three realms. And I want to be immortal.'

'I will make you the most powerful of all, but I cannot make you immortal. Death is important to maintain balance in creation.'

Tarakasura thought for a moment and said, 'If that is so, then I shall die by the hands of Shiva's son.'

Tarakasura knew that Shiva was mourning his wife Sati's death and was meditating in the Himalayas. The chances of him marrying again and producing a son were very low indeed. So Tarakasura felt safe.

Then followed years of misery for the gods. The all-powerful Tarakasura attacked and defeated gods, destroyed the hermitages of sages, and wreaked havoc in the universe.

The gods went to Brahma. 'You have done it again! Every time you grant a boon, we suffer! Tarakasura is killing all the gods. There won't be any heaven anymore! Do something!'

'You know I can't change my boon. But there is a catch to it: Tarakasura can be killed by Shiva's son. So, go to Shiva for help!'

The gods went to Shiva, but he was deep in meditation. They were scared to disturb him, as they knew his temper. They wondered what to do.

Himavana's daughter Parvati was Sati reborn. It was decided that Parvati would go to Shiva's abode and look after him while he meditated. The idea behind it was that whenever Shiva would open his eyes, he would see Parvati and recognize his Sati in her. They would get married and have a son.

To make the plan failproof, the gods also deputed Kamadeva, the god of love, to wait for the moment when Shiva opened his eyes and then shoot an arrow of desire at him. This would ensure Shiva falling in love with Parvati.

WHO IS KAMADEVA?

Kamadeva, the god of love, is Brahma's son. He shoots arrows of flowers with a bow made of sugarcane. His favourite flowers are of ashoka tree, mango tree, jasmine, white lotus, and blue lotus. A cuckoo, a parrot, and honeybees are his constant companions!

Ultimately, this elaborate plan worked. Shiva and Parvati got married. After some time, they had a son called Kartikeya. The gods did not wait for him to grow up into a young man and made him the commander-in-chief of their army when he was just seven years old!

With Kartikeya leading, the army of gods descended on Earth to fight Tarakasura.

'Ha! Look at the gods hiding behind a little child! Such cowards!' The mighty demon marched forth with his vast army of demons, ready to destroy Kartikeya and his army of gods.

The two armies met on the land between the rivers Ganga and Yamuna. In a short while, the battlefield was full of dead bodies.

Tarakasura was ignoring Kartikeya as he thought him to be a child, but soon he was going to change his mind!

'Come and attack me, you bully demon! Are you scared of a mere child?' Kartikeya challenged Tarakasura.

Tarakasura laughed and turned towards him. 'Do you want to be squashed under my feet, you little insect!'

Kartikeya jumped and attacked Tarakasura with his spear. Though he fought bravely, the mighty demon's head was finally sliced off by the little one's spear. The demons lost the battle to the gods.

> **DID YOU KNOW?**
>
> Kartikeya's vehicle is a peacock named Paravani.

Brahma's boon had looked after Tarakasura for many years but failed to protect him in the end. It was Tarakasura's own arrogance that brought about his death through the little loophole left in the boon.

Ganesha, the Most Worshipped God

Shiva lived with his wife Parvati on Mount Kailash in the Himalayas. As he was away for long periods of time to meditate, and Kartikeya was busy being the commander-in-chief of gods' army, Parvati was mostly alone at home and spent time with her friends.

On one such occasion, Parvati's friends suggested that she should also have an attendant like Shiva did. Shiva had many attendants, called ganas, who followed him everywhere. Parvati had none. Even Shiva's mount, the divine bull Nandi, was also always with him, looking after him. Parvati had no such person with her. So, she liked the idea of having her own personal gana or attendant.

Parvati took the sandal-turmeric paste that she used for bathing and made a little boy out of it, like a clay doll. Then she breathed life into it. Lo! A gana was created! Satisfied with her creation, Parvati went for a bath and told the little gana not to allow anyone to enter her rooms under any circumstances. It was a simple enough instruction, or so it seemed...till it created havoc!

Shiva returned home after a long trip. He tried to meet Parvati, but there was this unknown little boy guarding her door. He refused to allow Shiva entry to his own wife's rooms! Shiva tried to reason with the boy, explaining that he was Parvati's husband, but in vain.

'I am Parvati Maa's son. I have been asked by her to guard her door, and not let anyone enter, which is what I'm doing. I have not been told about you, so you will have to wait for her to come out. Please let me do my duty.' The boy gave an equally reasonable response. He had no intention to allow a stranger dressed in tiger-skin with snakes slithering over his body to enter Parvati's rooms, even though he claimed to be her husband!

'Son? I'm Parvati's husband and I don't know about you! Why should I believe you? I need to ask her myself!' Shiva was rightfully angry.

'Whether you believe me or not, you will still have to wait for her to come out, to ask her anything,' the boy said calmly.

Nandi and the ganas could not tolerate Shiva being insulted like this, and that too by a child! They attacked the boy. But the boy tackled them all by himself—very easily!

Seeing that he was no ordinary boy, a furious Shiva beheaded him with his trishula—the divine trident!

By then Parvati had finished her bath. She had heard the commotion, so she came out. The sight of her gana lying headless enraged her so much that she decided to destroy all creation!

'That was my son whom you have beheaded! I created him!' She burst out reproaching Shiva. His happy homecoming turned out to be far from happy!

Shiva tried telling her that he did not know that the boy was Parvati's son, which made him his son, too. It was an honest mistake! But Parvati was in no mood to calm down.

She summoned hundreds of ferocious multi-armed goddesses, Shaktis, and instructed them to attack the gaṅas and the gods. The Shaktis began to eliminate the gods, resulting in Brahma and Vishnu rushing to Shiva, telling him to resolve the situation fast! Then they pleaded with Parvati to stop the Shaktis.

'I will withdraw the Shaktis, but I want my son to be brought back to life,' said Parvati.

'I will put his head back on his body and make him alive!' Shiva declared.

Parvati withdrew the Shaktis. For a moment, it seemed that the situation was resolved, but no, it wasn't!

As luck would have it, before Shiva could do anything, a huge bird picked up the boy's severed head in its curved beak and flew off!

'I will go down to Earth and bring back a freshly severed head of some young boy,' Shiva assured his inconsolable wife.

Unfortunately, when he descended on Earth, Shiva failed to find any human head that had just been severed from the body. All he could find was the head of a young elephant.

'Well, something is better than nothing!' he told Parvati, as he fitted the elephant's head on the headless body of their son.

The boy came to life, but Parvati was still upset. 'People will laugh at his elephant head!' she cried.

DID YOU KNOW?

Just like his brother Kartikeya has a peacock for a vehicle, Ganesha has a mouse!

Shiva wanted his wife to be happy. 'Tell me, what else should I do to set this matter right? I will do anything for you and our son!' he promised.

'I want you to declare that our son must be worshipped before all other deities. Gods and humans must show him respect. No holy ritual should begin without praying to him first.'

'So be it!' declared Shiva, relieved that Parvati was finally appeased.

Since Parvati had created him as a gana, Shiva made the young elephant-headed boy the lord of all the ganas—gana-isha—or Ganesha.

This is how, even before he got his name, Ganesha received a boon from his father, Shiva.

And because of this boon, even today, Ganesha's name is the first name to be uttered when starting any important or auspicious task, be it laying the foundation stone of a building or performing any religious ritual or even opening a shop or an office to start the day. He is the most worshipped god of all gods.

Tripurasura's Boon, A Menace for the Universe

Demon Tarakasura had three sons—Tarakaksha, Vidyunmali, and Kamalaksha. The trio of asuras or demons was also called Tripurasura.

After Kartikeya's killing of their father, the sons panicked. They got together to find a way of protecting themselves.

'We should attack the gods! After all, we are the powerful sons of a powerful father. Together, we can beat them,' said one.

'We might be as powerful as our father, but not more than him. If Kartikeya can kill our father, we too will be killed easily,' the other reasoned.

'Let us pray to Brahma like our father did and ask for a boon of protection,' suggested the third one.

The last idea appealed to the three brothers, and they went to Mount Meru to perform penance. As time passed, they increased the severity of their penance. First, they stood on one leg and meditated and then they stood on their heads to meditate. The brothers continued praying for a thousand years.

Finally, Brahma was pleased with their efforts and the severity of the penance. 'What do you want from me?' he asked the three brothers.

'Please grant us immortality,' the demon brothers spoke in unison.

Brahma told them that invincibility was possible but not immortality, as all life in the universe had to eventually end.

The brothers said, 'In that case, grant us three fort-cities to live in. They should surpass even the cities of gods, and have the ability to roam about freely in the three realms.' Tarakaksha wanted a golden city, Kamalaksha a silver one, and Vidyunmali asked for one of iron.

Brahma agreed, but the brothers had more conditions to add.

'Let our three cities move freely in space, in separate orbits. Every thousand years, our cities should join at a place, for us to meet. After the meeting, we would go about our separate ways, for another

thousand years. And the only way we would die would be if some god would destroy all the three cities when they are joined together, with a single arrow.'

The boon sounded extremely peculiar to Brahma, but he granted it anyway. Mayasura, a famed demon architect, was deputed to build the cities. Each city was like a little kingdom. The three demon brothers happily ruled over their own independent little kingdoms, travelling through the three realms of heaven, Earth, and the netherworld. The cities, together known as Tripura, were self-sufficient and fully equipped with palaces, houses, and gardens. The demons living in them began to flourish and were happy.

The gods did not like it at all!

They went to Brahma, but he could not help them as he was the one responsible for giving those cities to the demon brothers!

The gods then went to Shiva. 'The demons are doing nothing wrong. I don't understand why you are so bothered!' was his response.

Finally, the gods went to Vishnu. He said, 'It's true, the demons are doing nothing wrong. Since this seems to be the problem then the solution will be to make them do wrong! The demons will have to be persuaded to become sinners.'

How to do that?

Vishnu created a man and taught him a new religion that did not believe in the existence of heaven or hell. He sent the man to the three cities to teach the demons this new religion, following which, they would end up getting confused and would start sinning.

Vishnu's plan was successful.

By now, the demon brothers had become bored with their simple lives. They were easily convinced about the new religion being preached by Vishnu's man. Even sage Narada was convinced! In fact, he went and told King Vidyunmali about the new religion. If an ardent disciple of Vishnu like Narada was speaking highly about something, it meant a lot! Others followed.

The result was that the demons decided to be adventurous! The Tripurasura started unleashing havoc on gods and mortals. Knowing that they could not die easily, that they were protected by Brahma's boon, they went on troubling everyone for nearly a thousand years.

Ultimately the king of the gods, Indra went to Brahma with the request of doing something to control the three demon brothers, considering it was his boon that had made them so powerful.

'I cannot modify my boon. You must go to Shiva for help.'

Indra, with all the gods, went to Shiva, and discussed their problem. 'The demons have become evil and should be destroyed.'

This time it was true. But then, Brahma's boon had made it very tough to destroy the Tripurasura. Indra had the support of all the gods in heaven, and all the beasts had also joined in. They needed someone as fierce and powerful as Shiva to undertake the execution.

Shiva agreed to destroy Tripura, but on the condition that he be made the lord of all the beasts (pashu), or Pashupati.

Preparations were made. All the gods shared half their power

FATHER WORSHIPS SON!

As Shiva's divine chariot raced towards the place from where he was supposed to shoot and destroy Tripura, its axle broke! That's when Shiva remembered that he had not worshipped Ganesha before starting this important task. Ganesha might be his son, but his own boon was applicable to him, too. It was only when Shiva had prayed to Ganesha that his chariot could move ahead!

with Shiva to make his trident (trishula) more powerful. Shiva made the mountain of Mandara his bow, serpent Vasuki the string of the bow, and Vishnu his arrow. He installed Agni at the tip and Vayu at the bottom of the arrow. The divine engineer Vishwakarma built a special chariot for him with sun and moon as its two wheels. Brahma became his charioteer. All the celestial beings and gods accompanied Shiva, armed with diverse weapons.

The thousand years of the three cities were reaching an end; the time came for them to align in a straight line as a single Tripura.

The moment the three cities joined, Shiva split them by using his trishula. Then he immediately shot his most destructive arrow called Pashupatastra into the three cities. The cities exploded in one go, destroying Tarakaksha, Vidyunmali and Kamalaksha along with countless demons. The menace created by Brahma's boon was finally over!

Shiva was henceforth named Tripurari or the destroyer of three cities, as well as Pashupati or the lord of all beasts.

So, while Tarakasura died at the hands of Shiva's son, his own sons died at the hands of Shiva himself.

Ravana's Birth, Boon and Curse

Vishwakarma was a master craftsman, a divine architect and engineer. He had built a capital for himself in the ocean beyond the southern tip of Bharat Varsha. It was a fortress kingdom on an island called Lanka.

But his happiness was short lived. Demon brothers Malyavan, Sumali, and Mali captured it from him, ruling the kingdom jointly for some time.

As their newly acquired kingdom flourished, the brothers became vain and ambitious.

'We have become very powerful...the most powerful in the entire universe!' Malyavan haughtily declared one day.

'You are right brother. Let's go out there and conquer more kingdoms.' Mali agreed with his brother.

'Let's attack heaven! We can easily defeat the gods and rule heaven too.' Sumali's ambitions had started soaring already.

'Yes! It is high time we did that!'

The brothers attacked heaven. And as it happened in every crisis, the gods rushed to Vishnu for help. After all, it was his responsibility to preserve the universe created by Brahma!

Vishnu fought and defeated the three brothers, who were too embarrassed to even return home, and went to netherworld instead. Since they were very powerful, they soon dominated netherworld. And

Sumali, the most intelligent of the three, became the king. Though he was happy ruling netherworld, Sumali still harboured the pain of defeat in his heart.

Meanwhile on Earth, sage Vishrava, the grandson of Brahma, had become very famous. Through intense meditation and yogic practices, he had acquired such immense powers that anyone with a young daughter wanted him as his son-in-law!

Bharadwaja, another very learned scholar, one of the Saptarishis or seven great sages, was much impressed with Vishrava and offered his daughter Ilavida's hand in marriage to him.

Ilavida and Vishrava led a happy married life. They had a son called Kubera and life seemed pleasant...but sadly, not for long.

In the netherworld, demon-king Sumali had a beautiful daughter Kaikashi, and he was looking for a suitable groom for her. Like all fathers, he wanted the best for his daughter.

He rejected all the kings. 'I am more powerful than any of the kings on Earth. My daughter will marry someone who is as powerful as me, if not more!'

Sumali started searching among the sages. They were known to have exceptional powers, yet they were not interested in ruling any kingdom, so he would be safe.

'A sage will never fight with me for my kingdom. Instead, he will father powerful sons to rule the world.'

Sage Vishrava's popularity had reached netherworld too. Sumali decided that Vishrava would be the best match for his daughter, regardless of him being married.

'Kaikashi, my beautiful daughter, get ready to seek sage Vishrava. I have chosen him to be your husband. He will give you powerful sons who will rule the world one day!'

It was easier said than done. Vishrava was already happily married and had a son too. He would not just leave everything and follow Kaikashi...or wait...would he?

One evening, as Vishrava was returning home, he met demon-princess Kaikashi on the way. No, it was not a chance meeting.

Demons also have mystical powers like the sages, and Sumali had tracked Vishrava's movements. He knew when the sage would be alone and sent his daughter at that very moment to meet him.

In the golden glow of the setting sun, Kaikashi looked like a goddess bathed in gold.

'O holy sage, I have come all the way only to marry you. Kindly marry me and bless me with powerful sons.'

Though mesmerized by her beauty, Vishrava hesitated...just for a bit.

'Evening is not the right time for granting a boon, especially of having sons.'

'I don't care! I have left my home for you; you must grant me the boon right now!'

'So be it! My boon will give you three sons and one daughter. But, since you are a demon-princess, your children will also be demons.'

'But I don't want demon sons!' Kaikashi cried.

'You wanted powerful sons, didn't you? Your sons would be very powerful indeed!' But then, Vishrava relented a bit and declared that her youngest son would not have any demonic qualities.

Thereafter, Vishrava and Kaikashi got married and lived together happily to fructify the boons. As promised by Vishrava, they had three sons and a daughter. The two sons were Ravana and Kumbhakarna, followed by daughter Surpanakha and finally, the youngest son Vibhishana, who was virtuous like his father.

Vishrava's first wife Ilavida's son Kubera grew up to become the king of Lanka. But eventually, his half-brother Ravana fought and defeated him, becoming the most powerful demon-king in the universe, making his grandfather Sumali very proud indeed.

Clearly, it was Sumali's thirst for avenging his defeat that led to Ravana's birth through sage Vishrava's boon.

The fight between the good and evil continued. Ravana was eventually killed by Vishnu's incarnation Rama. Since Kumbhakarna also died in the battle, Ravana's brother Vibhishana took over the reign of Lanka.

So, in the end, through his daughter Kaikashi, Sumali fulfilled his desire of getting his heirs to rule the kingdom he had lost. And since Vibhishana was a virtuous ruler, it was a victory of good over evil—a win-win for all!

Going back to Ravana's birth, though he was looked upon as a mighty demon-king, he was the son of a learned sage, who in turn was the grandson of Brahma, the creator himself. That's a strong lineage indeed!

Though his birth was the result of Vishrava's boon, why was Ravana born at all?

According to Hindu mythology, there is always a reason for everything that happens in the universe, including birth and death.

Ravana's birth also had a reason. Let us see what it was.

Vishnu, the god of preservation, lives in Vaikuntha with his wife Lakshmi, the goddess of fortune. It is a place beyond heaven, where palaces are made of crystal and flying chariots made of jewels. Beautiful, fragrant flowers bloom everywhere, and wish-fulfilling trees blossom all the time. It's a place dreams are made of!

Vaikuntha is guarded by two gatekeepers—Jaya and Vijaya.

> **THE KINGS OF LANKA!**
>
> Malyavan, Sumali and Mali ruled Lanka for thousands of years till they were defeated by Vishnu.
> Kubera ruled till Ravana fought him and seized control of Lanka.
> Ravana ruled till he died fighting with Rama.
> Vibhishana ruled after Ravana's death, and being given the boon of immortality by Rama, he continues to rule ever since.

Their job was to stop people entering Vaikuntha. Once, they stopped the four Sanat Kumara, the child-like monks, from entering. Unfortunately, they did not know that the Sanat Kumara were in fact the first mind-born sons of Brahma!

As expected, a major commotion ensued. For their insolence, Jaya and Vijaya were cursed by the Sanat Kumara to be expelled from Vaikuntha and be born on Earth. Vishnu came out to see what the commotion was about. He made the doorkeepers realize their mistake and agreed on the punishment.

Jaya and Vijaya apologized profusely to the Sanat Kumara, but once given, the curse could not be revoked. So, Vishnu came to their help by giving them two options. He also promised that he would come to Earth himself and bring them back to Vaikuntha.

The first option was that Jaya and Vijaya could be born seven times as normal mortals and devotees of Vishnu. The second option was that they could be born three times, but as staunch enemies of Vishnu.

Since they wanted to get back to Vaikuntha as soon as possible, Jaya and Vijaya chose the latter.

The curse of their first birth was being born in the Sat Yuga as Hiranyaksha and Hiranyakashipu, killed by the Varaha and Narasimha avatars of Vishnu, respectively. The curse of the second birth was in the Treta Yuga, as Ravana and Kumbhakarna, killed by the Rama avatar of Vishnu. Finally, the curse of the third birth was in the Dwapar Yuga, as Dantavakra and Shishupala, to be killed by the Krishna avatar of Vishnu.

Though Jaya was cursed to be born as Ravana on Earth, his birth happened through the boon of sage Vishrava!

Ravana's Boons, With Loopholes

Ravana was a brahmasura, which means he was half brahmin, half demon. His father was sage Vishrava, and mother was Kaikashi, a demon princess.

He had an elder half-brother Kubera, with whom he competed in all the fields, just like siblings normally do. Ravana was a bright student and did well in studies as well as in the art of warfare.

'You have learnt all the scriptures so fast! I am proud of you, my son.' Getting praised by his father always made young Ravana very happy.

Not as competitive as his younger half-brother, Kubera completed his studies and went off to meditate. His intense meditation pleased Brahma immensely. Always happy to grant boons, the creator blessed Kubera with a lot of wealth and a grand flying chariot called Pushpak.

> **DID YOU KNOW?**
>
> Ravana was an exceptional poet, musician and scholar. He authored *Ravana Samhita*, a book on Vedic astrology and *Arka Prakasham*, a book on Siddha medicine and treatment.

Meanwhile, Vishnu had defeated demon brothers Malyavan, Sumali, and Mali, long back. And till now, he was still looking for a suitable person to rule Lanka.

Seeing Kubera being blessed with immense wealth by Brahma, Vishnu decided to hand over the task of ruling the island-kingdom of Lanka to him.

Kubera used his wealth to develop Lanka into a golden city, the grandest in the universe.

Seeing Kubera's name and fame, Kaikashi pushed her children, especially Ravana, to pray to Brahma and ask for a similar, if not bigger, boon.

'Follow your elder brother's footsteps. Go, and do a severe penance for Brahma. When he is pleased, ask him for a boon of immense strength to overcome your enemies.'

Brahma was the lord of creation, and it was within his power to grant any person immortality if he wanted to...so Ravana believed.

Ravana prayed so hard that Brahma had to reward him with a boon.

'Make me immortal, O Lord.' Ravana was very clear in his demand.

Brahma shook his head. 'That is not possible! It is against the law of nature. Whoever is born, must die. I cannot change the law of nature for anyone.'

'Since you cannot make me immortal, then give me the nectar of immortality that the gods possess.' Ravana was adamant.

Though Brahma realized how dangerous it was to grant such a boon to Ravana, he could do nothing about it.

'Granted! Instead of immortality, I will bless you with an alternative of concentrating your life in your navel, making you the most powerful demon in the universe. I will also give you the power of changing your physical form at will.'

However, Ravana was far from being fully satisfied. 'I have one more request. Give me the boon that no god, demon, heavenly spirit, serpent, or wild beast can kill me.'

Brahma agreed to this. The boon was granted.

Ravana had not included human beings in his list, as they were too weak in his opinion. It was this error of judgment that cleared the path for Vishnu to take the human incarnation of Rama, to kill Ravana in the future.

On getting blessed with miraculous powers, the first thing Ravana did was to attack Kubera, dethrone him and make Lanka his own kingdom. He even took possession of the divine flying chariot Pushpak.

Soon, Ravana became the king of Lanka. The kingdom flourished under his rule and began to be known as the city of gold. But even that was not enough for him.

'I have received the greatest boons from Brahma. I am invincible! But I cannot be satisfied with a small island. I want to rule the entire Earth...why just the Earth...I want to rule all the three worlds!'

Ravana's reign of terror started. He attacked kingdoms and destroyed them, since the kings were no match for him. Brahma's boon was helping Ravana. He looted all the wealth of the kingdoms and took away the women he liked to his kingdom in Lanka.

The earth was trembling under the destructive power of demon-king Ravana.

After creating terror on Earth, Ravana decided to show his invincibility to gods by attacking them. The first one in his sight was Yama, the god of death. Conquering Yama was a great idea and Ravana couldn't wait to defeat him.

'Once I make the god of death bow to me, no one in the three worlds would dare to oppose me!'

Yama was surprised to see a huge army making its way towards his palace, headed by Ravana. 'Be ready guards! We are under attack!'

Yama's guards were confused. Who would be so crazy to fight with the god of death? It was like inviting death to themselves!

Ravana fought well, slowly and steadily destroying the army of Yama. Seeing the massacre, Yama decided to face Ravana himself. He took his Kaladanda, the weapon of death, and stepped on to the battlefield.

Just as he was about to fire the weapon, Brahma suddenly appeared in front of Yama, blocking him.

'Do not fire the weapon, son!' he said.

Yama could not believe his eyes. He thought maybe Ravana was playing some trick! Why would Brahma stop him from killing Ravana, knowing well what sort of a menace he had become to everyone? So, he turned his attention to Ravana again, aiming his Kaladanda at him.

Brahma stepped forward. 'No! Don't do this! If you do it, you will turn me into a liar!'

Yama stopped. His Kaladanda, the ultimate weapon of destruction, was also a boon from Brahma. He could not go against his wishes.

'I have given the boon to Ravana that he cannot be defeated by any god. If you fire the Kaladanda at him and he dies because that's my boon to that weapon, then it will make my boon to Ravana false. If

Ravana does not die because of my boon to him, then my boon to your Kaladanda would become false. Either way, I will become a liar!'

This was a difficult situation indeed! Yama had to stop the war and go away.

Ravana looked around in pride. 'Instead of giving me a fight, the fool ran away!' He laughed, and declared, 'I am Ravana, the conqueror of Yama!'

Again, conquering the god of death was not enough for him. Ravana's greed was truly a bottomless pit. Nothing seemed to fill it! He had already asked enough from Brahma. There was nothing more he could get from him. Ravana knew that. So, who else could he go to now?

Ravana decided to seek Shiva's help.

It was not easy to get Shiva's attention by mere penance. So, Ravana attempted to lift Mount Kailash, Shiva's abode. The great mountain trembled. So, Shiva pressed his right toe on the ground, crushing Ravana beneath it.

A trapped Ravana composed and sang hymns in praise of Shiva for a long time, but in vain. Then he found a unique way to get Shiva's attention. He chopped his head!

TEN HEADS OF RAVANA

Ravana's ten heads symbolize his knowledge of the six shastras and four vedas. But as his hunger for power grew, Ravana's ten heads of knowledge began to symbolize the ten qualities of lust, anger, delusion, greed, pride, envy, intellect, mind, will, and ego.

Ravana chopped his head and offered it to Shiva! Not once, but nine times. When he did it for the tenth time, Shiva appeared. 'You have everything, O Ravana, what do you want now?'

'Immortality!'

'I cannot grant you that, but I can grant you the boon of acquiring all the celestial weapons.' With this, Shiva also restored the nine heads of Ravana.

Brahma's boon of miraculous powers and Shiva's boon of celestial weapons had surely made Ravana invincible, if not immortal.

With his divine boons, Ravana became drunk with power and ruthlessly created havoc in the universe. Little did he know that the tiny little loophole that was left in his boon of invincibility, would be the hole from where Rama, a human, would enter to kill him!

Curses on Ravana, Mapping His Life

Ravana had become quite a tyrant with all the power and weapons that he had acquired through his boons. Most people were afraid of him. But there were some who were not afraid to curse him for his atrocities.

One such brave person was King Anaranya of Ayodhya. He did not submit to Ravana like other kings did. He chose to fight instead! Ravana used his celestial weapons to defeat the king.

But before dying, Anaranya cursed Ravana. 'You will be killed by a prince from my clan!' The clan was Suryavansha.

There was another curse to reaffirm this.

Once, Ravana had asked sage Vasishtha to become his teacher. The sage was not willing. Arrogant Ravana could not tolerate anyone refusing him, and hence, he imprisoned the sage. King Kuvalayasva managed to rescue Vasishtha, but not without the latter cursing the king of Lanka.

'You and your family will be destroyed by a member of this very Suryavansha clan whose king has rescued me!'

King Kuvalayasva belonged to Suryavansha, as did Rama, who eventually vanquished Ravana.

There was another sage who cursed Ravana.

Sage Maudgalya was once sitting in a swastika pose, a yogic posture where he rested his neck on his yogadanda, a short wooden stick with a handle. Ravana came across the sage meditating in this odd posture and tapped the yogadanda with his chandrahasa, the celestial sword gifted by Shiva. The stick broke and Maudgalya fell, breaking his back.

Furious, he cursed Ravana. 'This chandrahasa of yours will cease to be effective in future!'

Ravana was unable to use the celestial sword of Shiva after this. One powerful celestial weapon was wasted!

There were other people too, who did not tolerate Ravana's misbehaviour and cursed him. One of them was Nandi, Shiva's mount and gatekeeper.

Once Ravana was flying in his Pushpak and came across Mount Kailash. To his irritation, he realized that his divine flying chariot was unable to cross the mountain! The mountain was no ordinary one, it was the abode of Shiva and Parvati. It could not be crossed by anyone!

Believing that he was the most powerful person in the universe, Ravana could not tolerate this obstruction on his path. He started shouting and Nandi came out to investigate.

'This is Lord Shiva's abode, and no one can disturb him. Please take another route.'

Seeing Nandi the bull, Ravana laughed, making fun of him. 'Who are you to tell me what to do? Just look at yourself, you monkey-faced bull!'

Deeply hurt, Nandi cursed Ravana, 'You and your entire clan will be destroyed by monkeys one day. Just wait and watch!'

The curse came to fruition when Hanuman, the monkey-faced god and his army of monkeys destroyed Ravana's clan and his army in the battle fought between Rama and Ravana in Lanka.

Ravana was also known for his aggressive conquests of women. He had several wives, as well as a harem, where he brought women—captured over the course of his many travels. This habit of his, ultimately led him to be cursed by some women.

Vedavati was one such strong woman who fought and cursed Ravana. She was the daughter of sage Kushadhwaja.

During one of his travels, Ravana saw Vedavati sitting deeply engrossed in meditation. Attracted by her beauty, he offered to marry her. Vedavati refused. Ravana could not handle this rejection from a woman and grabbed her hair. As he dragged her forcibly, the furious Vedavati fought back, cursing him, 'I will return and be the cause of your death!'

Then she leaped into the sacred fire-pit immolating herself.

Vedavati was born as Sita and became the cause of Ravana's death through his fight with her husband Rama.

Even Surpanakha, Ravana's own sister, cursed him!

Surpanakha had secretly married Vidyutjihva, a danava. Though danavas were also demons like rakshasas, they were mortal enemies of each other. Ravana being a rakshasa was enraged with this match. It resulted in a battle, where Surpanakha's husband was killed by her own brother!

'I can never forgive you for killing my husband. I will not kill you myself, but I will certainly be the cause of your death!' Surpanakha cursed. And in fact, she was the one who started it all!

Feeling lonely, Surpanakha started looking for a husband for herself. During one of her visits to Panchavati, in the forests of southern India, she met Rama and Lakshmana. When they rejected her proposal of marriage, she turned to attack Sita in anger. Lakshmana was quick to prevent the attack, cutting off Surpanakha's nose and ears in the process.

A humiliated Surpanakha reported the matter to her brother Ravana, instigating him to take revenge. This is when Ravana decided to kidnap Sita, which eventually led to his downfall.

Ravana was also cursed by his own nephew, Nalakubera, the son of Kubera.

Kubera and his family lived in Alakapuri, up in the north of Bharat Varsha, after being ousted by Ravana from Lanka. Though they were half-brothers, they had stopped having a cordial relationship after Ravana showed his demonic behaviour.

Ravana couldn't care less. His only concern was to remain the most powerful king in the universe, and he continued to flaunt his power by terrorizing people. When he travelled, people got out of his way in fear.

One day, while travelling in his flying chariot Pushpak, Ravana caught sight of a beautiful woman. She was heading towards Alakapuri.

'Who is this beautiful woman, who seems unaware that I'm travelling across the sky! She has not even as much as glanced at me or my grand Pushpak!'

The woman was apsara Rambha, one of the best dancers of Indra's court. But now she was married to Nalakubera, Kubera's son.

That day she was on her way to Alakapuri. Lost in the thoughts of her beloved, she did not notice Ravana's Pushpak flying past. It was not a deliberate thing on her part; it just happened!

Why would Ravana want to believe that anyone in the entire universe could be so engrossed in their own thoughts, as to not notice him! He felt insulted.

Turning back his Pushpak, he followed Rambha and grabbed her.

'Let go of me! I am going to my husband Nalakubera.'

'You are not going anywhere. You are coming with me!' Ravana pulled Rambha over to his chariot.

'No! How can you touch me like this? I am your nephew's wife, your brother's daughter-in-law!'

'Huh! You are nobody's wife! You are an apsara, a dancing girl of gods. You needn't have only one husband; you can have many!'

WHAT IS AN APSARA?

Apsaras are fairy-like celestial dancers. They fly from one place to another. Mostly they stay in heaven, but occasionally they come to Earth as well. They are always very beautiful and never grow old.

Rambha somehow managed to escape Ravana's clutches and reached home in a state of shock.

The moment Nalakubera learnt how his uncle had treated his wife, he rushed to Ravana in anger. 'How dare you touch my wife like that?'

'Like what? She's a dancing girl and it's her job to please all men.'

'No, she is not a dancing girl anymore! She is my wife. She told you that and yet you did not listen to her pleas. I curse you that if you ever touch a woman against her wish, your head will shatter into countless pieces!'

Since curses—like boons—always come true, this curse became the reason why Ravana was always scared to misbehave with any woman after this incident. It was Nalakubera's curse on Ravana that protected Sita when she was in his captivity in Lanka.

Even after being blessed with powerful boons, Ravana's misdeeds resulted in so many curses, which eventually paved the way towards his end.

Curse on Harini, Birth of Dasharatha

One day, Indra saw sage Trinabindu engaged in rigorous penance, and this bothered him. He decided to trouble him. Why would Indra be bothered, one might ask.

Indra was highly insecure about his kingship of Indraloka. He was always worried that someone—anyone—would do harsh penance to please the godheads and ask for the boon of becoming the king of gods. So, he disrupted the meditations of kings, sages, and even demons. And to do this job for him, Indra used the celestial entertainers.

Harini was a beautiful apsara, a celestial dancer in Indra's court.

'Harini, I want you to go where sage Trinabindu is meditating. He has been sitting there for far too long! Go, sing and dance in front of him, around him, to the point that he opens his eyes. Use all your skills to distract and disturb him!' Indra commanded.

Like the other apsaras of Indra's court, Harini was a gifted singer and dancer. Using her skills, she successfully disturbed Trinabindu's

DID YOU KNOW?

Celestial entertainers, apsaras, and gandharvas, were bound by the rules of Indra, the king of gods. They could be sent anywhere to entertain anyone, as directed by their master. There were no complaints, because being a celestial entertainer had its benefits, too. They were not only immortal but looked young and beautiful forever!

meditation. And anyone can guess what happened next: the sage got furious. And as is well known, furious sages tend to curse.

'You have no respect for a sage! You will be born as a woman on Earth to learn how to treat people according to their stature!' cursed sage Trinabindu.

'Please have pity on me...I am an apsara. I live in heaven. Life on Earth will be intolerable for me!' Harini pleaded.

'You should have thought about it before disturbing me!' Trinabindu's anger remained unabated.

'I had no personal intention of disturbing you, please believe me. I was just following the orders of our king, Indra...' Harini was in tears now.

Trinabindu's heart melted. 'I cannot take my curse back but can modify it a bit. While on Earth, if celestial flowers touch your body, you will be freed from the curse.'

Harini was relieved. She was aware that sages, gods, goddesses, and celestial musicians kept travelling from heaven to Earth and back. Someone was bound to carry heavenly flowers, and there was a good chance that they might drop them. She was quite optimistic!

> **WHO WAS TRINABINDU?**
>
> **Sage Trinabindu,** who cursed Harini, was the grandfather of sage Vishrava, Ravana's father. Small world!

Soon after, Harini was born as Indumati, the daughter of King Bhoja of Vidarbha. She grew up to be as beautiful as an apsara. But she had no memory of her life as Harini. As was the norm in those times, Bhoja held a swayamvara for his daughter, which was attended by many kings and princes.

Swayamvara is an event where a woman chooses her own husband from amongst many suitors. Princess Indumati fell in love with the young and handsome prince of Kosala, Aja. She chose him as her husband, and they left for Ayodhya, Kosala's capital.

Indumati was blissfully happy with her husband. They had a son, Nemi.

Old king Raghu of Kosala was very happy to have a grandson. 'Now that you have become a father to a bonny prince, I think it is my time to retire from kingly duties. I, therefore, hand over the reins of this kingdom to you, my son.'

Raghu handed over the kingdom to Aja and spent his time playing with his grandson. King Aja proved to be an able ruler, just like his father. Things were going well, or so it seemed.

Aja and Indumati were deeply in love with each other and tried to spend as much time together as possible. One fine day, they were taking a walk in the royal gardens. At the same time, sage Narada was passing by above, on one of his usual travels across the realms. He carried a celestial garland of flowers wound around his veena, a stringed musical instrument.

Unfortunately, as Narada bent forward to look at the handsome royal couple, the garland slipped off the veena and fell towards Earth.

Oops! The garland fell on Indumati! And the moment it touched her, she fell down unconscious! Trinabindu's words came true. Harini was released from her curse and returned to heaven, leaving behind the senseless body of Indumati.

Meanwhile, King Aja was shocked beyond words. 'How delicate she must be for the flowers to kill her!' he cried inconsolably. He continued to cry for days, when finally, sage Vasishtha sent his disciples to console him. The disciples explained the story of Indumati being apsara Harini and why she had to return to heaven. Her time on Earth was limited.

Aja could not recover from his heartbreak. He fell sick and eventually died. But before dying, he saw to it that his son Prince Nemi was well-trained in the art of ruling the kingdom and was crowned as his successor. Aja spent his last days on the banks of river Sarayu, leaving the kingdom in the hands of young Nemi.

Nemi grew up to be a very powerful king—so much so, that he was once requested by Indra to fight a mighty demon, Sambara, who had attacked heaven. Sambara assumed ten identical forms and attacked Nemi from ten different directions. Nemi turned and twisted his chariot in all the ten directions at the same time, killing the ten Sambaras.

From that day onwards, Nemi came to be known as Dasharatha, or the one who can control ten chariots or rathas simultaneously.

Harini's curse resulted in her coming to Earth and giving birth to one of the most valiant kings of Kosala, Dasharatha, the father of Rama.

Curse on Dasharatha, Turning Into a Boon

Dasharatha was the king of Kosala, a flourishing kingdom, with its capital Ayodhya on the banks of river Sarayu. He was a brave and just king, loved by his people. Everyone in his kingdom was happy, except Dasharatha himself. Why was that?

In ancient times, it was normal for kings to have multiple wives and many children. Dasharatha had three wives, too, but no sons. He had a daughter though, but she was not considered an heir to the throne. (Those were the times when only sons inherited their father's kingdom.) So, the cause of Dasharatha's sadness lay in him being heirless.

One day, Dasharatha went to the forest near river Sarayu to hunt. Hunting was his favourite pastime, as it was of all the kings.

Dasharatha was a good archer and had mastered the difficult technique of shabdavedi. It was the art of listening to the sound made by any animal and killing it without seeing, from a distance. This technique helped him to become one of the best hunters in his kingdom.

That fateful day, as Dasharatha stood near the riverbank, he heard what he believed to be the sound of an animal drinking water. He shot an arrow in the direction from which the sound came. Confident of his success, he started walking towards where he expected the injured animal to be. However, what happened next was a tragedy.

'Who has shot me to death? Who has hunted me like an animal?' A man's voice cried from a distance, from the very spot where Dasharatha had shot his arrow.

With a sinking heart, Dasharatha rushed to see what had happened. To his shock, he saw a young man lying in agony along the riverbank, a fatal arrow piercing his chest! There was a half-filled pot of water beside him.

Dasharatha could see his own blunder. He mistook the sound of the pot being filled up with water to be that of an animal drinking water. A deadly mistake indeed!

'You seem to be from a royal family...yet you have hunted me like an animal! I was going to carry water for my old, blind parents. They are helpless without me. What will happen to them once I'm dead?'

The young man writhed in pain. Dasharatha fell at his feet, begging for forgiveness. He explained how it was an accident.

The young boy was called Shravana Kumar. He was taking his blind parents on a pilgrimage. They were waiting for him nearby, while he went down to the river to get water for them.

'O King, take this pot of water to my thirsty parents who must be waiting for me. Tell my father what you have done and ask for his forgiveness. I forgive you since you hit me by mistake. But my father's forgiveness is more important. I have lost only my life, he has lost much more.'

Dasharatha lifted Shravana in his arms and went to where his parents sat waiting.

As he gave water to the old couple, they thought their son had returned and started chiding him fondly. 'What happened son? Why are you so late? We were getting worried about your safety. This is a forest after all!'

Expecting Shravana to respond, they were surprised to hear Dasharatha, who gave them the tragic news. The couple was shocked and heartbroken.

'If you had not admitted your guilt, my anger would have caused your head to explode! Take us to our son, immediately!' the father said.

Dasharatha led them gently to where he had laid Shravana. The couple mourned their son and performed his last rites.

'I curse you to suffer a death like mine! You will die when your son is taken away from you.' Cursing thus, Shravana's father held his wife's hand and entered the funeral pyre of their son.

This heart-wrenching incident haunted Dasharatha for years. However, as time passed, a realization dawned upon him. 'Shravana's father's curse on me is perhaps a blessing in disguise. For the curse to come true, I must have a son!'

Excited with the prospect of having an heir, Dasharatha called the royal priests and discussed the matter. They advised him to conduct a fire sacrifice called Putrakameshti yagya. Pleased, the gods blessed him with four sons. Queen Kaushalya had Rama, Queen Sumitra had twin sons Lakshmana and Shatrughna and the youngest, Queen Kaikeyi had Bharata.

Dasharatha had managed to turn the curse around into a boon, or so it seemed for a while at least. It was many years later that the forgotten curse came to fruition. How so?

The four princes of Ayodhya grew up to become brave teenagers. They were well versed in all the subjects including warfare. It was time now for King Dasharatha to announce the crown prince. Though everyone knew Rama to be their next king, a formal announcement was required as per norms of the times.

MANTHARA'S REVENGE!

Once, when little Rama was playing with a ball and stick, Manthara threw the ball far away. An angry Rama struck her on the knee, injuring her badly. Since that time, Manthara disliked Rama. Getting him exiled was her way of getting her revenge!

While preparations were going on in the palace to celebrate the forthcoming announcement, Kaikeyi's attendant Manthara decided to change the story. She reminded her mistress of an old incident where Dasharatha had granted two boons to Kaikeyi.

Long ago, when Dasharatha was fighting the celestial battle with demons, Kaikeyi was his charioteer. During the battle, the chariot's wheel broke, and an arrow pierced through Dasharatha's armour into his chest. At that time, Kaikeyi the charioteer quickly repaired the broken wheel and drove the chariot away from the battlefield. She nursed the wounded Dasharatha back to health. In gratitude, the king offered her two boons.

'I wish for nothing now, except to look after you. Maybe I will ask for these boons later in life,' she had said.

'Now is the time to ask for those boons. Get your son Bharata to be the crown prince,' urged Manthara.

Her idea seemed great to Kaikeyi!

So Kaikeyi asked Dasharatha for her two boons right before he could announce the crown prince's name. She demanded that her son Bharata be crowned as king and Rama be exiled to the forest for fourteen years.

Boons must be respected. The unsuspecting Dasharatha, bound by the boons he had granted, had no choice but to comply. The joyful occasion turned into a tragic one, as Rama, the would-be crown prince, left Ayodhya with his wife Sita and younger brother Lakshmana.

The forgotten curse of Shravana's father came to fruition. Dasharatha's heart could not endure the separation from his beloved son, and he passed away. Just before closing his eyes, burdened by the weight of his past actions, the king revealed the curse to his wife Kaushalya.

DID YOU KNOW?

Shravana Kumar's parents were blind hermits. When they became old, Shravana took them for a pilgrimage to all the holy places. Since he could not afford transport, he carried them on his shoulders in two baskets, hung on the two ends of a bamboo pole.

'When a person does good things, he reaps good things. Likewise, when a person does wrong, he reaps its effects too. I wronged Shravana's parents. Today I am facing the consequences,' Dasharatha murmured with his last breath.

This is a story where the curse briefly turns into a boon, before going back to its original form.

Curse on Tadaka, Rama's First Battle

Suketu was a yaksha, a nature spirit. He had no children. Brahma being the creator, Suketu decided to pray to him. He did severe penance and performed a yagya, a sacred ritual to invoke divine powers.

Suketu's devotion and dedication finally attracted the attention of Brahma, who appeared before him.

'Please bless me with a child, as strong as a thousand elephants,' Suketu pleaded with folded palms.

Brahma had to grant the boon, but he became thoughtful. He could foresee the potential consequences of granting such immense power to a son. 'If I give him such a powerful son he is sure to cause havoc on Earth. Maybe I should give him a daughter, who would be less likely to cause trouble.'

Little did Brahma know what girls were capable of!

'Suketu, you shall be blessed with a daughter soon. She'll be as powerful as she'll be beautiful.'

WHAT IS A YAKSHA?

A **yaksha** or yakshini is a nature spirit of trees, forests and water bodies, the angel guardians of wilderness. They live under the earth in the Himalayas, guarding the wealth of the planet. Kubera is the king of yakshas.

So, Suketu was blessed with a beautiful daughter. He named her Tadaka. She grew up to be a powerful young woman. She fell in love with demon Sunda and married him. They lived a happy life, and in course of time, had two sons—Mareecha and Subahu.

One fateful day, Suketu and his son-in-law Sunda ventured into the forest and happened to come across sage Agastya. Unlike other sages, Agastya was short and squat.

Suketu could not resist making fun of the sage's physical appearance. 'Have you ever seen such a funny looking creature? Oh no, he is a man! He is a dwarf!'

Suketu laughed and Sunda joined in heartily, unaware of the consequences that would follow.

Agastya could not tolerate this insult, and in a fit of rage, cursed them, 'May both of you meet your end!'

Sage Agastya's words, like piercing arrows, took immediate effect. Suketu and Sunda fell lifeless!

Tadaka could not believe her eyes...both her father and husband were dead! Just like that! Overcome with grief and anger, she rushed to attack sage Agastya.

The sage was ready. He immediately cursed Tadaka as well, but no, not to die. It was much worse! 'You shall transform into a ferocious demoness, feeding on human flesh. Your sons, too, shall become demons!'

With the curse taking effect, Tadaka transformed from a charming woman to a grotesque demoness with bulging fiery eyes, thick matted hair and yellow fang-like teeth. She rushed to the netherworld to seek demon-king Sumali's advice.

'Go to Lanka. My grandson Ravana will surely help a fellow-demon's widow.'

Ravana helped Tadaka capture the cities of Malada and Karusha on the banks of river Sarayu. The powerful demoness with the strength of a thousand elephants destroyed the cities and established her own forest Tadakavana.

The anger of losing her father and husband had not left Tadaka. She took it out on the people living around her and became a menace, especially to the sages. Her demon sons, Mareecha and Subahu, were no better. They would spare no opportunity to harass the sages by throwing blood, flesh, and bones into the sacred fires of their yagyas. In fact, they would not hesitate to even catch and devour the pilgrims passing through the forest!

News of the demons' atrocities reached sage Vishwamitra. Concerned about the safety of the hermitages and the people, he decided to seek help.

And so, Vishwamitra visited King Dasharatha in Ayodhya.

'I need your sons to help me get rid of the menace of demons in our forest,' the sage requested.

Dasharatha was surprised. His sons were too young. They had just returned home after completing their education in a gurukul.

'What can these youngsters do? Fighting demons would require other skills than mere archery. Let them get trained further...'

'No! They are fine as they are. I want to take Rama and Lakshmana with me for a few days. And don't worry, I will teach them how to use cosmic weapons,' said Vishwamitra, cutting the king short.

Dasharatha did not want to argue any further as he was aware of the sage's temper and tendency to curse.

WHO WAS VISHWAMITRA?

Sage Vishwamitra was King Kaushika of Kanyakubja kingdom, before he gave up everything to become a sage. He had many children, including Sushruta, the father of plastic surgery!

'Go and help the sages. Get rid of the demons. May the gods protect you, my sons.' Dasharatha blessed Rama and Lakshmana as they left with sage Vishwamitra.

On the way, the sage showed the princes how the once beautiful region had been turned into an eerie forest by the demoness.

'The time has come for Tadaka's end. She is the strongest demomess we have ever seen. You have to kill her!'

'Being a woman, how can Tadaka have such power?' Rama asked. And that is when Vishwamitra related the story of Suketu, and how Tadaka became a demoness.

'But how can we kill a woman? We have been taught to always protect them and never attack them!' Rama raised a valid point.

'She is not a woman, but an evil creature. Destroying her is necessary for the good of the people. And looking after the people's welfare is the duty of a king,' said Vishwamitra.

So, Rama and Lakshmana accompanied Vishwamitra to his hermitage. Under the guidance of the sage, the young princes underwent rigorous training, learning the art of using powerful cosmic weapons.

Once prepared, Rama twanged his bow to challenge Tadaka.

'Who dares to disturb my sleep? The fool deserves to be eaten alive!'

Tadaka rushed out raging from her cave in a cloud of dust. Seeing the two princes, she started raining stones and rocks on them. The entire forest trembled.

Undeterred, the brave brothers, armed with newfound skills, started shooting arrows at the giant demoness. Rama's arrows sliced off her arms and Lakshmana's arrows chopped her nose.

Using her magical powers, Tadaka assumed many forms. Sometimes she swooped from above, or attacked from behind, or just disappeared in a cloud of dust—screaming all the while. Even after losing her arms, she used sorcery to throw trees and boulders at the brothers.

Vishwamitra looked up at the sky and saw that the sun was about to set.

'The day is about to end, Rama. Remember that demons grow stronger after dusk. So, just strike to kill her!' advised Vishwamitra.

Following the sage's instruction, Rama released arrows capable of sriking an invisible target by following the sound. They pierced the demoness, who, assuming a giant form, rushed at the brothers. Rama shot a thunderbolt arrow, piercing her heart. With an ear-shattering scream, Tadaka fell down—dead.

The sages sighed in relief as the menace of Tadaka finally ended. The animals and birds emerged from their hiding places. The forest rustled as leaves and flowers appeared on the trees.

'Tadaka was blessed to be slain by you, Rama. You freed her from her curse. She will not be a demoness any more.'

In Hindu mytholgy, when a person meets their end through Vishnu, they go to heaven. Rama, being Vishnu's incarnation, helped Tadaka in getting rid of her curse and returning to heaven.

Little did Rama and Lakshmana know that killing Tadaka was the first of many such battles they would be fighting in future!

Kubera Curses, Rama Releases

Sage Kashyapa had many wives. One of them was Pradha. Her sons were gandharvas or celestial singers. Tumburu was one of them.

Tumburu was considered the best singer amongst the gandharvas in heaven and hence was much in demand at Indra's court. All the celestial dancers wanted to dance only on Tumburu's songs. They also wanted to learn music from him. Tumburu loved all this attention!

Fame travels fast. Kubera the god of wealth, residing in Alakapuri, also heard about Tumburu's exceptional musical skills.

'Get that singing gandharva to perform at my court!' Kubera ordered.

So, Tumburu sang for Kubera. And kept on singing... At the end of the concert, both of them had become friends.

'Why don't you stay here and teach my apsaras and gandharvas? Look at all the wealth around you! You will be treated well,' said Kubera.

Kubera wanted Tumburu to sing for him every day and give music lessons to his courtiers as well. But this was not possible.

'I have my duty towards Indra. I cannot leave his court like that. But what I can do is come as often as

DID YOU KNOW?

Alakapuri is the capital of Kubera, the king of yakshas. **Amravati** is the capital if Indra, the king of gods. **Brahmaloka** is where Brahma lives. Vishnu lives in **Vaikuntha** and Shiva lives in **Kailash**.

I can and spend as much time with you as possible.'

Kubera had to be satisfied with Tumburu's offer.

Time passed. Tumburu had started teaching the apsaras. Out of them, Rambha was his favourite. The singing gandharva and the dancing apsara made a great pair. Little did they know that their joy was short-lived!

One day Tumburu and Rambha were so engrossed in their singing and dancing that they lost track of time. They were due to perform at Kubera's court.

'Where is Tumburu? He was told to bring Rambha to my court. I can't wait for him all my life!' Kubera fumed.

By the time Tumburu reached Kubera's court with Rambha, Kubera had lost his patience and temper. 'For this lapse of yours, Tumburu, I curse you to be born as demon!'

As soon as he cursed the gandharva, Kubera regretted his words. Tumburu was his dear friend after all. But what was done was done. Curses could not be reversed.

'I am sorry for slipping in my task, but please, tell me how and when I would be liberated from this curse,' pleaded Tumburu.

'You will be liberated by Rama, Vishnu's incarnation on Earth. Then you will regain your gandharva form and return to heaven,' Kubera assured him.

Accordingly, Tumburu was born as demon Viradha to the giant demon Jaya and his wife Satahrada.

Viradha grew into a large pot-bellied fierce-looking demon, with two extra-ordinarily long arms, devouring any animal or human that came his way. He lived in Dandaka Forest, arousing fear in every living creature of that region.

One day, during his exile, Rama entered Dandaka Forest with his wife Sita and younger brother Lakshman. They were surprised to see the forest in shambles—trees were broken, shrubs were trampled, the water pools were undisturbed, and there were no birds singing!

'GRRRR....' A strange roar stopped the three in their tracks.

'It doesn't sound like any animal we know!'

Before they could discuss the sound any further, Rama saw a giant, monstrous looking creature creating the uproar. He was heading towards them! Wearing leopard skin, with lion, wolf, leopard, deer, and an elephant's head, caught pierced on an iron spear in his hand, the fierce demon looked like Yama.

'How dare you enter my forest? And that too with weapons and a woman! Don't you know I am Viradha and that this forest is my home, and the flesh of all living creatures is my food?'

The earth seemed to tremble when this giant demon spoke. The trees shook, as did Sita. Seeing their dazed looks, Viradha laughed, causing further trembling and shaking all around. Then like lightning, he grabbed Sita in one arm and swiped at the two brothers with his loaded spear.

'This fair woman shall be my wife!' Viradha declared.

Seething in anger, Rama and Lakshman attacked the demon with a swift volley of arrows.

'I have a boon from Brahma that protects me from any weapon on Earth. It is impossible to kill me with these puny arrows! Go! I will spare your lives! Just leave this beautiful woman behind,' Viradha said as he walked away with Sita.

This angered the two princes further and their attack became more intense. Viradha realized that the brothers were not scared of him. And they had no intention of leaving Sita with him either. This was very irritating, to say the least! No man had ever challenged Viradha before.

'You asked for it!' So saying, the giant demon let go of Sita and the loaded spear. He immediately grabbed the two brothers in his two arms instead!

Rama and Lakshmana continued to attack Viradha valiantly, but in vain. Placing them on his shoulders, the demon let out a loud roar and strode off into the deep dark forest.

'Help, someone please help us! Rama, the heir to the throne of Ayodhya and Lakshmana, both sons of the great king Dasharatha, are being taken away by a giant demon! I will now become the meal of hungry tigers and bears!' Sita started crying loudly, hoping of getting some help. 'Eat me, O nasty demon! Spare the sons of Dasharatha!'

Hearing his wife's cries, her offering herself to the demon to save the brothers, pushed Rama's anger to such a point that he managed to break off Viradha's right arm. Lakshmana did the same with the demon's left arm.

The demon fell on to the ground like a tree struck by lightning. Not only losing his arms, but Sita's words also succeeded in stopping the demon from going any further.

'Dig a pit Lakshmana. This demon cannot be killed by weapons, so we will bury him alive!' Rama was very angry indeed!

'My release is at hand!' Viradha thought happily. 'Didn't Kubera say that Rama would free me from the curse!'

'In my ignorance and arrogance, I did not recognize you, O son of Dasharatha. But now I feel blessed to have met you, for you alone can relieve me from this curse. Please hear me out!'

Rama and Lakshmana stopped digging the pit and turned to listen to the demon's story. Viradha told them about his earlier life as Tumburu the gandharva and Kubera's curse.

'So you see, you have to bury me in a pit for me to leave this life and go back to being the gandharva that I was.'

The brothers dug a deep pit and buried a very grateful Viradha in it. Finally, Tumburu was released from Kubera's curse, and he went back to his world of gandharvas and apsaras.

Curse on Vishvavasu, Helpful to Rama

Gandharva king Sri had a son named Vishvavasu. A handsome gandharva, a celestial musician of heaven, Vishvavasu once performed strict penance to please Brahma the creator. He wanted a boon of long life, but Brahma who was extraordinarily generous that day, blessed him with immortality instead!

Proud of this acquisition, Vishvavasu happily roamed around heaven enchanting various apsaras, the celestial dancers of Indra's court.

Indra the king of gods was not very pleased with this new-found swagger of Vishvavasu. The gandharvas, along with the apsaras, were supposed to perform in Indra's court to entertain him and his guests. But Vishvavasu had started ignoring his duties. He also became careless about being present in court on time.

One evening, as Vishvavasu strolled in later than usual, an angry Indra shouted at him. 'This behaviour is unacceptable! Why are you so late?'

'I was busy elsewhere...if you must know.' Vishvavasu replied and walked up arrogantly towards his designated seat.

'Such insolence! The way you are behaving, you do not deserve to live in heaven, let alone enter my court. You are only fit for being a demon!'

So cursing, Indra threw his vajra at the gandharva, who instantly turned into an ugly demon. Vishvavasu's head and thighs had squeezed into his body, with only one eye remaining visible.

DID YOU KNOW?

Vajra is the one of the most powerful weapons in the universe. It is Indra's weapon and was made from the bones of sage Dadhichi by Vishwakarma.

'What have you done!' the gandharva cried. 'How will I eat? How will I live?'

Indra promptly gave him two very long arms that could be extended to catch his prey from a distance. He also gave the demon a large mouth on his belly from where his long tongue hung out.

'From now on, you will be known as Kabandha (headless body). Now, get out of my court! Go and live with other demons!' Indra ordered.

'Mercy, O king! Mercy!'

On Kabandha's pleading, Indra added, 'You will be freed from this demonic life and return to your original form when Rama and Lakshmana sever your arms.'

Kabandha had no choice but to move out of heaven and go down to Earth and live in a forest. Since demons are carnivorous, Kabandha had to live in a forest where he could get plenty animals to eat. Though sometimes, like other demons, he would also eat men passing through the forest.

Kabandha started living in the forest called Krauncha.

It was not difficult for him to find a prey for himself. A look at Kabandha's demonic form was enough to scare an animal or human to death! He was as large as a mountain and as dark as a storm cloud with a voice like thunder. His single round yellow eye on the stomach glowed like fire, adding fierceness to his already fearsome looks.

So, Kabandha waited for Rama to come and release him from his curse. But then, nothing is ever so easy!

Why would Rama, who was the crown prince of Ayodhya, come to Krauncha Forest? Even if he did, how would Kabandha recognize him? Such thoughts would bother the demon a lot, but he had no other option but to continue waiting.

Finally, Kabandha's wait was over...but hold on, he did not know that yet!

Rama and his brother Lakshmana were looking for Sita, who had been kidnapped by Ravana. On the way, they met Jatayu, the king of vultures, who lay half-dead by a blow of Ravana's sword. The dying old vulture informed the brothers that Sita was abducted by Ravana in his flying chariot.

WHO WAS JATAYU?

Jatayu's father was Aruna, son of sage Kashyapa and Vinata. While Jatayu informed Rama about Sita being taken away by Ravana in his flying chariot, his elder brother Sampati used his supernatural vision to locate Sita in Lanka. Hence, both brothers helped Rama to find Sita!

After performing Jatayu's funeral, Rama and Lakshmana had to find a way to get to Ravana. They were passing through the Krauncha Forest, discussing how they should proceed next, when Kabandha saw them. No, he did not recognize them.

The monstrous demon blocked their way, as he did for any living creature passing through Krauncha. The peace-loving brothers were not scared at all. They just ignored the demon and took another path. They were engrossed in trying to solve their own problem of finding Sita.

'HALT!' Kabandha thundered.

The two brothers continued talking and walking, unperturbed. Little did they know that help was coming to them through this monstrous demon!

Feeling insulted, Kabandha threw out his long arms and caught the brothers—Rama in his right arm and Lakshmana in his left.

'So you think you can escape, huh?' he roared.

Rama and Lakshmana looked at each other. They were still not afraid! Lakshmana said to Rama, 'Brother, you go and find your wife. I will deal with this demon here.'

The two men did not even plead to be saved! Who were they? Kabandha was getting more and more irritated.

Since he was very hungry, he decided to swallow both men together. But the moment he pulled up his arms towards his mouth, Rama and Lakshmana quickly cut them off. Kabandha lost his balance and fell on the ground with a deafening thud.

'Who are you?' cried Kabandha.

Lakshmana introduced Rama and himself.

'Oh, I have been waiting for this very day all my life!' Kabandha said to the surprise of both the brothers. And then, he went on to narrate his story.

'Only you can relieve me from my curse, O Rama. Please light a fire and cremate me. I shall be eternally grateful.'

The two brothers made a huge fire and cremated him. And guess what happened!

Kabandha's demonic form melted, and out of the flames rose a handsome gandharva in his celestial form, dressed in spotless garments and jewels. It was Vishvavasu!

'Go to Rishyamook hill. There you will find monkey-king Sugreeva, who has lost his kingdom to his brother Vali. Help Sugreeva regain his kingdom and he will help you find your wife Sita,' he advised.

Before leaving for heaven, Vishvavasu also told the brothers how to reach Rishyamook. 'Go west till you reach lake Pampa in Matangavana, where sage Matanga's disciple, old Shabari, is waiting for Rama's blessings. To the east of Matangavana is Rishyamook hill, where Sugreeva lives in a cave.'

This is how a boon led to a curse, Brahma's boon and Indra's curse. And that curse helped Rama in meeting the people who assisted him in finding Sita.

Boons of Hanuman, His Invincibility

Punjikasthala, an apsara, lived in sage Brihaspati's hermitage. One day, she went beyond the boundary of the hermitage, looking for flowers. The further she went, the more beautiful flowers she saw!

Pleased with her discovery, Punjikasthala started filling up her basket with colourful fragrant flowers, when she heard some people talking. Curious to find out who they were, she went closer.

To her surprise, she saw a couple of young handsome men talking and laughing. They seemed to be enjoying themselves! Till now she had only seen stern sages and their equally serious-looking disciples at the hermitage.

Punjikasthala did not know that these young men were gandharvas. She was so mesmerized by the sight, that she just stayed there hidden behind the bushes, watching them.

When she did not return to the hermitage for a long time, Brihaspati and his disciples decided to look for her. And they found her soon enough!

WHO WAS BRIHASPATI?

Sage **Brihaspati** was Brahma's grandson. He was the teacher or guru of the gods, while sage Shukra was the guru of demons. Since he was the teacher of gods, Brihaspati is also considered as a god.

The sight of Punjikasthala engrossed in watching the gandharvas, enraged the sage so much that he cursed her.

'This is how monkeys behave! You do not deserve to live in my hermitage. You shall be born on Earth as a monkey!'

The poor apsara was aghast. She apologized profusely and pleaded for mercy. But, as is well known, a curse cannot be taken back. Sage Brihaspati relented and said that once Punjikasthala had a baby, she would be free of the curse.

Punjikasthala was born on Earth as Anjana, daughter of monkey chief Kunjara. She grew up to marry monkey king Kesari.

One day, while roaming the hills of Kishkindha, Kesari found a silver bowl with some rice pudding (kheer). He took it for his wife Anjana, who happily ate it.

It was a very special rice pudding, as it carried Vishnu's blessings. Let us see how...

King Dasharatha of Ayodhya performed a grand Putrakameshti yagya, a fire-sacrifice, at the end of which, Agni the fire-God appeared with a bowl of rice pudding blessed by Lord Vishnu. That pudding was meant for Dasharatha's three wives. After eating the pudding, they were to give birth to sons.

Kaushalya and Kaikeyi had their share but as Dasharatha was handing over the bowl to Sumitra, a bird swooped down and snatched the bowl away. The other two queens shared their pudding with Sumitra, resulting in her giving birth to twins Lakshmana and Shatrughna. Kaushalya gave birth to Rama, and Kaikeyi to Bharata.

So, it was this blessed pudding that reached Anjana, and she gave birth to a son, Anjaneya, also known as Hanuman. It's worth noting that sage Brihaspati's curse ultimately resulted in the birth of Hanuman!

But how did the bowl of rice pudding reach Kishkindha from Ayodhya?

The bird who had snatched the bowl was Suvarchala, a cursed apsara, who was freed of her curse the moment she touched the sacred bowl. As the apsara returned to heaven, the bowl fell down to Earth.

At that moment Anjana was praying to Shiva, asking to be blessed by a son. Shiva told Pavan the wind-God to blow the pudding bowl to Kishkindha. And that is how Kesari found it! Since Pavan was the carrier of the blessed pudding, he was considered as the father of Hanuman. Hence, Hanuman is also called Pavan-putra or son of Pavan.

Little Hanuman or Anjaneya as he was called then, was a naughty child, as boys of that age are. One day, he was very hungry, and his mother was nowhere in sight. He looked around but could not find anything to eat. Suddenly he saw the rising sun through the window. Round and red-coloured, it almost looked like some fruit to little Anjaneya. He leaped out, arm outstretched, to pluck it from the sky.

Unknown to him, Anjaneya's leaps covered huge distances. Surya the sun-God first took it to be a child playing, till he saw Anjaneya catching up with him! He shouted for help. Indra the king of gods, riding his divine white elephant Airavata, rushed to save Surya.

Plump and fair, Airavata appeared yet another fruit to Anjaneya! He lost interest in Surya and moved towards Airavata. To save his elephant and himself, Indra hurled his divine weapon vajra at Anjaneya. The vajra hit the monkey-child on his jaw and he fell lifeless.

Seeing Anjaneya lying lifeless, an enraged Pavan stopped flowing. With no air, the living beings on Earth started dying. The worried gods rushed to pacify Pavan.

Shiva resuscitated little Anjaneya, blessing him with the boon that he would not be harmed by his weapons.

Since it was Indra's vajra that injured Anjaneya, he gave him the name Hanuman, which in Sanskrit, means the one with a disfigured (mana) jaw (hanu). And the boon he gave was that Hanuman's body will be as strong as Indra's vajra, and henceforth, the vajra would not be able to affect him.

Surya the sun-God, because of whom this entire incident happened, shared one per cent of his energy as a boon with Hanuman. Brahma gave the boon that Hanuman could take any form he wished and travel anywhere he wanted to at high speeds, and that he would have the power to induce fear in his enemies and destroy fear in his friends.

Fire-God Agni gave the boon that fire will not harm him. Varuna the water-God gave the boon that water will not harm him. Yama, the God of death, gave the boon that Hanuman will not be affected by his Kaladanda or the rod of punishment. Vishwakarma, the divine architect, gave the boon that Hanuman would be safe from all the objects of his creation, which included many divine weapons and chariots.

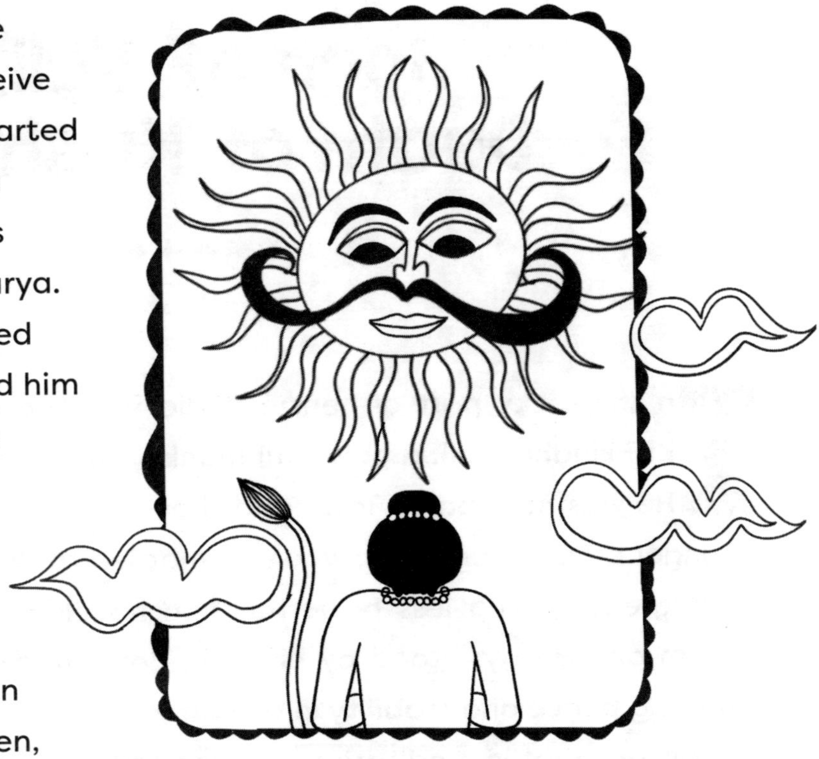

When it was time for Hanuman to receive education, Kesari started looking around for a suitable teacher. His search led him to Surya.

Kesari approached Surya and requested him to accept Hanuman as his student. But Surya was hesitant. He remembered the incident of Hanuman chasing him! But then, Hanuman was so persistent that Surya could not refuse. There was still a little problem though. Surya was always on the move! How would the teaching arrangement work? Hanuman found a solution to it by positioning himself opposite Surya and travelling with him, learning his lessons on the go!

Hanuman was a brilliant student and mastered the scriptures very soon. Surya blessed him with the boons of Laghima and Garima, that enabled him to reduce and increase his size phenomenally.

Born from a curse, it were the boons received from gods that made Hanuman invincible and immortal.

Boon of Vali, Death of Krishna

In the rocky part of central India was the monkey kingdom of Kishkindha. Vali, a powerful monkey, was the king of Kishkindha. He was married to Tara, and they had a son, Angad. Vali had a younger brother Sugreeva, who was married to Ruma.

Sugreeva being less powerful than his elder brother was in awe of him and always stood by his side. Both made an effective team, ensuring peace and stability in the kingdom.

Vali once sat in meditation for a long time. It pleased Lord Brahma, who offered him a boon. Vali wanted that in any duel, his opponent should lose half his strength to him. Brahma granted the boon. Vali was already extremely powerful; now he became invincible!

When Ravana heard about Vali's new-found strength, he immediately wanted to test it. He knew that Vali meditated for long hours. So one day, when Vali was sitting in deep meditation, Ravana slyly went up to him from the back. Vali sensed him coming but did not move.

Ravana got closer. Vali immediately caught him in one arm, trapped him under the other, and then continued his meditation; Ravana was pressed in his armpit for hours! Ravana could not bear the insult and pain for long and so he sought forgiveness. Vali immediately released Ravana, demonstrating that he was the most powerful being on Earth!

Once a mighty buffalo demon named Dundubhi challenged Vali to a duel. Dundubhi was as tall as a mountain, had the strength of a thousand elephants and looked fearsome with sharp horns. Vali seized the buffalo demon by the horns, swirled him around, threw him down, and crushed him to death. Then holding his lifeless body by the tail, flung it away with such force that it flew miles away and landed right into the hermitage of sage Matanga, on Rishyamook hill. The hermitage got splattered with blood.

'You have dirtied my hermitage with blood!' exclaimed Matanga and cursed Vali. 'If you ever set foot here, your skull will break into a thousand pieces!'

Powerful as he was, Vali could never go to Rishyamook hill after that.

Blessed with Brahma's boon, Vali continued to rule his kingdom well...till a bitter feud with his brother Sugreeva changed the course of their lives.

After Dundubhi's death, his brother Mayavi decided to avenge him. He went up to the gates of Kishkindha and roared, 'I will kill you Vali! Come out and fight!'

Vali rushed out to meet the challenge, followed by his brother Sugreeva. Seeing the two strong monkey brothers rushing to attack him scared Mayavi. He lost courage and ran away to the nearby forest. Vali and Sugreeva followed him.

Mayavi tried to fight with Vali, but was unsuccessful. He then fled into a cave. Before following him into the cave, Vali instructed Sugreeva to keep watch.

'If I fail and Mayavi comes out of the cave, you must kill him!'

Sugreeva waited and waited. No one came out of the cave. After a very long time, blood came out of the cave's entrance, and demonic screams could be heard. Sugreeva took it to mean that Vali had died at the hands of the demon. He closed the cave with a large boulder, went back to Kishkindha and declared himself as king.

But Vali was very much alive! It was he who had killed Mayavi, and that was why the demon had been screaming. When he made his way to the cave entrance, Vali discovered it to be closed.

'Sugreeva, what have you done?' he shouted.

Raging in anger, Vali smashed the boulder and rushed to his palace, only to see Sugreeva on the throne! Vali thought his brother had betrayed him. Sugreeva tried to explain his actions, but Vali would not listen. He felt that Sugreeva had not waited for him, and had blocked the cave's entrance to prevent him from coming out. So, he threw Sugreeva out of his kingdom and took away his wife Ruma for himself!

Sugreeva ran off to Rishyamook hill, the only place Vali could not enter because of Matanga's curse. He was accompanied by his chief minister Hanuman and a few other faithful monkeys.

One day, all of them were sitting on a hilltop, when they saw a demon in a flying chariot carrying off a weeping woman. She was throwing down her ornaments. The monkeys picked them up.

Soon Rama and Lakshmana, the exiled princes of Ayodhya, came there looking for Rama's missing wife Sita. The monkeys showed them the ornaments that they had picked up. Rama recognized them to be Sita's.

Sugreeva promised to help Rama in finding Sita. He told Rama the story of how his own brother Vali had thrown him out and had taken away his wife Ruma.

'Don't worry, my friend,' Rama put his hand on Sugreeva's shoulder.

'Just like Vali has taken away your wife Ruma, Ravana has taken away my wife from me. I understand how you feel and will help get rid of Vali for you.'

Rama and Sugreeva made a plan.

Because of Brahma's boon, facing Vali in a fight would have meant Rama losing half his strength. It was decided that Rama would shoot from a hiding place, while Sugreeva would fight Vali.

Sugreeva went up to Kishkindha and called Vali out to fight, while Rama hid in a nearby plantain grove.

DID YOU KNOW?

Vali's father was Indra and **Sugreeva's** father, Surya. They had a common mother, Aruni. When Rama left Earth, Sugreeva decided to leave too and went back to his father Surya, after crowning Angad as the king of Kishkindha.

Vali came rushing out. 'Challenging me, you puny fellow?' He fell upon Sugreeva. Holding each other around the waist, each trying to throw the other on the ground.

'But which one is Vali and which one is Sugreeva?' wondered Rama, too confused to shoot. They looked almost identical! Sugreeva returned, hopelessly beaten by Vali, accusing Rama of letting him down. Rama explained his confusion and sent Sugreeva back with a flower garland around his neck.

'That fool Sugreeva has not learnt his lesson!' Vali laughed as the duel started again. This time Rama had no difficulty in telling one from the other. He shot at Vali while he was engrossed in the fight with Sugreeva.

Vali died and Sugreeva mounted the throne of Kishkindha. Vali's son Angad was made the crown prince.

Since he had killed Vali while hiding, Rama blessed Vali to kill him when he took the incarnation of Krishna. Consequently, in the next birth, Vali was born as Jara the hunter and killed Krishna with his arrow, shooting from behind the bushes.

Whether gods or demons, everyone must face the consequences of their own actions.

Vandin's Boon Saves Ashtavakra's Father

Sage Uddalaka Aruni was a very learned sage. He had a daughter named Sujata and a son named Shvetaketu. The sage taught the Vedas to young disciples, who came from across the region to his hermitage to study. Kahoda was one of his students.

'You are the best among my disciples and my favourite student, Kahoda. I feel that there can be no better husband for my daughter than you.'

Kahoda and Sujata got married and lived in a hut in Uddalaka's hermitage. Kahoda joined his father-in-law in teaching the Vedas to young students. Sujata would also sit amongst the students and listen to her father and husband teach the Vedas.

Sujata got pregnant, but she continued to attend the lessons. She would listen to the lessons with rapt attention. Unknown to her, the baby in her womb also did the same. Unfortunately, her husband Kahoda was not as good in the knowledge of the Vedas as her father Uddalaka.

WHO WAS UDDALAKA ARUNI?

Sage Uddalaka Aruni was the first natural scientist in the world! According to him, three powerful elements—heat, water, and food—make up all living things. He also gave birth to Indian atomism, with his belief that particles, too small to be seen, mass together to make the physical universe.

One day, while reciting the Vedas, Kahoda made a mistake. The baby in Sujata's womb squirmed and kicked. 'Father, I have learnt the mantra you are chanting. The way you are saying it is wrong!' he called out.

Stunned and embarrassed, Kahoda went on reciting the Vedas. He made another mistake, and again the baby pointed it out. This happened seven times. Kahoda would say something wrong, and the baby would say its correct version.

When this happened the eighth time, Kahoda could not bear it anymore! He cursed his unborn son, 'Such arrogance in a person who is not even born yet! I curse you to be born bent; not once or twice, but eight times!'

When the baby was born, he was indeed a misshapen bundle of bones. Since he was bent (vakra) in eight (asht) places, he was named

Ashtavakra. Although his body was bent, Ashtavakra's brain was very sharp. In fact, he was quite a prodigy; he learnt Sanskrit and understood the philosophy of scriptures, much before anyone else in the hermitage.

Those days, King Janaka of Mithila was holding debates in his court, where the winners were being rewarded. Janaka was Sita's father.

Kahoda decided to go to Mithila and earn some money. Being Uddalaka's student, he was confident that he would be able win several debates in King Janaka's court and make good money.

In his over-confidence, Kahoda did not bother to find out anything else about the debates. He had no idea what he was getting into!

King Janaka had a court scholar called Vandin who loved to debate and send the losers to drown in river Ganga. Kahoda was no match for him. Like many other scholars before him, he also lost to Vandin in a debate and was sentenced to be drowned.

Meanwhile, Ashtavakra grew up in the hermitage, assuming his grandfather Uddalaka to be his father. He took young Shvetaketu to be his elder brother.

One day, the two boys went to bathe in the river. As it happens with young boys, they got into an argument. Soon it escalated, and Shvetaketu blurted out that Ashtavakra had no father! It had the desired effect. The argument stopped abruptly, as Ashtavakra was stunned by this information.

He ran back to the hermitage to confront his mother. 'Where is my father? What happened to him? Why is he not returning?'

Sujata could not hide the truth from her young son anymore. 'Your father lost to Vandin in a debate held at King Janaka's court and was punished by drowning.'

Ashtavakra decided to avenge his father's death. Barely twelve years old, he left for Mithila. On reaching Janaka's palace, he was stopped by the guards.

'Go away boy! Only learned brahmins and scholars are allowed to enter King Janaka's assembly.'

'Years and grey hair do not make a person learned. I am well versed in the scriptures. Please allow me to meet the king.' Ashtavakra managed to convince the guards.

> **KING JANAKA**
>
> **King Janaka** had a deep interest in scriptures and often discussed them with scholars. Impressed by Ashtavakra, Janaka invited him regularly and eventually became his devoted disciple.

'I have come to defeat Vandin in debate,' Ashtavakra announced as soon as he entered King Janaka's court.

The king was intrigued at the young boy's confidence. 'Young boy, answer my questions first, then you may debate with Vandin.'

King Janaka then asked, 'What is that which does not close its eyes when asleep? What is it that which does not move when born? What is it that which has no heart? What increases its own speed?'

Without wasting a moment, Ashtavakra answered, 'Fish, egg, stone, and river.'

Janaka was impressed and welcomed him into his assembly for debate. After a long debate, Vandin conceded defeat.

'Punish him by drowning as he punished my father!' Ashtavakra declared.

It was then that Vandin told him, 'I am the son of Varuna, the lord of all waterbodies. My father has been conducting a yagya under water for over twelve years and needed learned scholars for that. Your father is alive, as are the other scholars, who were drowned.'

'Since you have won the debate, you may ask me for any boon,' he added.

Ashtavakra asked for his father and all the other scholars to be returned to their families.

Now that Vandin had lost to Ashtavakra, he returned to his abode and all the 'drowned' scholars returned to life, including Kahoda.

The son whom the father cursed because of his superior knowledge ultimately saved his father using the very same knowledge!

On the way back to the hermitage, Kahoda repented for cursing his son and took him to bathe in river Samanga, daughter of Ganga. Ashtavakra came out of the water, fully cured of his deformities!

Curse of Durvasa, Birth of Bharata

A very learned sage, Durvasa was respected by all in heaven and on Earth, but because of his temper, everyone feared him. When angry, he would spare no one, not even his wife!

One day, sage Durvasa visited the hermitage of sage Kanva, unannounced, which was also a habit of his. Kanva was not there. At the entrance sat a girl, lost in her thoughts. She was so absorbed in her own world that she did not even notice Durvasa entering the hermitage. Obviously, the sage was not greeted or welcomed the way he expected.

'Who is this insolent girl who did not get up and bow to me in respect? Doesn't she know who I am?' the angry sage thundered.

The young girl was Shakuntala, the foster daughter of sage Kanva. Why was she lost in her thoughts?

It so happened that King Dushyanta of Hastinapur was once hunting in the forest when he struck a fawn. The injured fawn fled to sage Kanva's hermitage. Dushyanta followed it there and saw Shakuntala and her friends watering plants. The girls also saw him.

WHO WAS SHAKUNTALA?

Shakuntala was the daughter of sage Vishwamitra and apsara Menaka but was abandoned by her mother on the banks of river Malini. Sage Kanva found the baby surrounded by Shakunta birds and named her Shakuntala.

Shakuntala was apsara Menaka's daughter and was as beautiful as her mother. Dushyanta fell in love with her, and so did she with him. He forgot about the injured fawn or that he was out for a hunt. The king stayed back in the hermitage. He and Shakuntala got married.

Sage Kanva had still not returned.

Dushyanta was waiting for the sage, to take his permission and blessings before taking Shakuntala to his capital as his wife. Unfortunately, after some time, he was called for some urgent work in his capital and had to leave without meeting sage Kanva.

King Dushyanta had given his signet ring to Shakuntala before leaving for his palace, promising to return soon to take her with him after getting her foster father's blessings.

Since then, Shakuntala kept on thinking of Dushyanta and waited for him. That was the reason why she had not noticed Durvasa on his arrival and hence could not welcome him. She was totally lost in her thoughts!

Durvasa did not wait to find out the reason for Shakuntala's behaviour. He felt insulted and lost his temper. And as usual, immediately cursed Shakuntala. 'The one you are thinking of so much, whose thoughts made you forget to welcome me, that person will forget you!'

Hearing Durvasa's voice, Shakuntala snapped out of her reverie instantly and got up to bow

DID YOU KNOW?

Sage Durvasa's wife, **Kandali**, often quarreled with him, and in a heated argument, he cursed her to turn to dust. Regretting his action, he transformed the dust into a tree, blessing it to bear fruit yearly and become essential in rituals. Thus, the banana tree was born, and its fruit, kadaliphalam, became a sacred offering to the gods.

to the sage respectfully.

'I apologize for not noticing you...it will not happen again.'

The apology did not help at all, as it confirmed the fact that sage Durvasa's entry into the hermitage indeed went unnoticed.

As he was leaving in rage, one of Shakuntala's friends rushed after Durvasa to explain the reason behind her distracted state of mind. The sage realized that his intense anger was not justified. Since he could not retract his curse, he modified it, 'The person who forgot Shakuntala will recall her again if she shows him a personal token of his.'

Shakuntala was relieved. 'I have this ring that Dushyanta gave to me. In case he really does not recognize me, I could show him this.' She showed the large signet ring of Dushyanta, that she wore on a thread around her neck, to her friends.

Poor Shakuntala did not know that the damage was already done!

Time passed. Sage Kanva had returned but Dushyanta still had not. Shakuntala was pregnant. Kanva suggested that she should not wait for her husband anymore. She should go to Hastinapur herself to meet him.

Shakuntala set off for Hastinapur to meet Dushyanta. On the way, there was a river to be crossed by boat. Shakuntala stopped at the riverbank to rest and refresh herself. While she was washing herself in the cool clear water of the river, unknown to her, Dushyanta's signet ring slipped off and fell into it. Durvasa's curse was taking its effect!

Shakuntala reached the capital and the royal palace. When she met King Dushyanta, he failed to recognize her. He had completely forgotten everything about his visit to Kanva's hermitage! She tried to remind him that they had married and searched for his signet ring as a proof. It was missing! That's when she realized that she had lost it somehow on the way. Since she had nothing else to show him, Shakuntala left the palace feeling humiliated and heartbroken.

Shakuntala was returning to her hermitage when her mother apsara Menaka met her on the way. Menaka was a celestial being. She had seen everything that was happening with her daughter. She decided to take Shakuntala away with her to sage Kashyapa's hermitage.

In time, Shakuntala had a son. She named him Bharata. He was taught and trained by the best of teachers. Bharata grew up to be brave and fearless, subduing even the wildest of animals easily.

Meanwhile, a fisherman was surprised to discover the royal signet ring in the belly of a fish that he had caught. He took the ring to the palace. Seeing the ring, Dushyanta's memories of Shakuntala and sage Kanva's hermitage came flooding back. He immediately set off for the hermitage. But Shakuntala was not there. Dushyanta returned disappointed.

Years later, King Dushyanta went hunting again. He came across a shocking scene—a young boy was counting a lion's teeth by opening his mouth!

'Who are you young boy? I would like to meet the parents of such a bold and strong boy as you!' Dushyanta couldn't help but ask. Imagine his surprise when the boy told him that he was Bharata, the son of King Dushyanta!

Bharata took Dushyanta to meet his mother, Shakuntala. And the family was reunited. Such was the trouble Durvasa's curse had caused!

Bharata grew up to be a powerful king on whose name the country was named Bharat Varsha. He was also the ancestor of the Pandavas and the Kauravas.

Curse on Vasus, Birth of Bhishma

The attendant deities of Indra are the eight elemental gods known as Vasus. They are Anala, Anila, Soma, Ahas, Dhara, Dhruva, Pratyoosha, and Prabhasa.

One day, the Vasus, with their wives, were visiting the forest on Mount Meru. They were having a nice time when Prabhasa's wife spotted a divine cow. It was the wish-fulfilling cow named Nandini.

Nandini belonged to sage Vasishtha, who had a hermitage on Mount Meru. The cow was in a habit of roaming the woods surrounding the hermitage.

Prabhasa's wife requested her husband, 'I want this divine cow. Please do anything and get it for me!'

> **NANDINI THE COW**
>
> **Nandini** was a beautiful, white, wish-fulfilling divine cow. Mother of all cows, she had the miraculous power of providing anything her master sage Vasishtha desired. But then, Vasishtha had no desires, so Nandini happily fulfilled the needs of his hermitage.

Prabhasa knew that the cow belonged to sage Vasishtha. He tried to reason with his wife, 'I will get you another cow, dear. I know the sage will refuse to part with this one.'

His wife did not agree. So Prabhasa, who was much in love with her, decided to steal the cow for her. He took the help of his brothers to do this task. So, the eight vasus stole Nandini and took her with them to heaven.

Sage Vasishtha was away when all this was happening. When he got back, he was surprised to see that Nandini had not returned home. It was unusual for her to be away from the hermitage for so long. He and his disciples searched the nearby forest, but in vain.

Using his yogic powers, sage Vasishtha found out what had happened. He was livid with rage and cursed the Vasus immediately.

'The arrogant Vasus have committed a grave sin of stealing a brahmin's property. May they take birth on Earth and suffer the pain of mortals!'

When the Vasus came to know of the curse, they rushed down to the sage's hermitage, feeling sorry. Apologizing profusely, they begged him to revoke his curse. At last sage Vasishtha relented.

'I cannot take back my curse, but I can modify it,' he said. Turning to Prabhasa, he continued, 'Since you instigated your brothers to commit the sin, they will not suffer mortal lives for long, but you will.'

The eight Vasus then went to goddess Ganga, seeking her help to get an early release from their forthcoming mortal lives. She promised to bear them as her sons in her mortal incarnation, which she was due to take because of Brahma's curse.

Why did Brahma curse Ganga?

Once, King Mahabhishek of the Solar dynasty visited Brahmalok to worship Brahma. Ganga was also present in the court. Their eyes met and they fell in love. Being in Brahma's court, they could not say anything, so they just stared at each other.

Brahma did not like it. In his court, people were supposed to pay attention to him, not to anyone else. This was an insult!

'This is inappropriate behaviour! Both of you shall be born on Earth as mortals and go through the pains and pleasures of being human,' cursed Brahma.

Ganga was aghast at the curse and apologized profusely. Brahma's heart softened. 'I cannot take back the curse, but will modify it a bit. You will give birth to the eight Vasus and return to heaven.'

The story now shifts to Earth.

Mahabhishek was born as Shantanu, king of Hastinapur—a prosperous kingdom in northern India.

One day he was walking on the banks of river Ganga when he met goddess Ganga in her mortal incarnation. Being a goddess, she recognized Shantanu as Mahabhishek, though the king did not.

King Shantanu fell in love with Ganga, so much so, that he wanted to marry her! 'O beautiful lady, marry me and be my queen.'

Ganga agreed, but on the condition that Shantanu would never stop her from doing whatever she wanted to do. 'I will leave you, if you do so,' she added. It was a simple enough condition, or so the king thought, and agreed instantly.

King Shantanu and Queen Ganga lived happily for some time and then the queen was pregnant. The kingdom would get an heir. Everyone celebrated. But it was not to be!

Ganga gave birth to a son. But lo...she picked up the baby and went to river Ganga and dropped him in its waters! Shantanu had followed his wife quietly. To his horror, he saw his newborn son floating away in the swift flowing river!

The king recalled his promise to his wife and did not say anything. He did not want her to leave him. Soon they had another son. Ganga did the same with this one too. In fact, she did the same with her seven sons. By now, Shantanu had lost his patience.

When Ganga went to drop their eighth son into the river, Shantanu came out of hiding.

'What sort of a heartless woman are you to be killing your own sons!' he cried.

Queen Ganga stopped and then told her husband the story of the accursed Vasus. Their sons were those Vasus. Considering Shantanu had broken his promise, Ganga left him immediately, taking the eighth Vasu with her.

Shantanu, filled with grief from the loss of his wife and son, devoted his entire time in ruling his kingdom. He did not marry.

Years later, King Shantanu was walking along the banks of river Ganga, when he saw a strange sight. The swift flowing river's course

DID YOU KNOW?

As a Vasu, his love for a woman, his wife, drove Prabhasa to instigate his brothers into committing a crime. Hence, as a mortal, Bhishma was cursed never to experience the love of a woman in his life. In fact, his death also came about at the hands of a woman.

was being obstructed by arrows shot by a young handsome boy! The boy saw the king and disappeared.

Soon, he appeared again, this time with Ganga.

'This is our son Devavrata, the eighth Vasu. He has been taught the holy scriptures by sage Vasishtha and the art of warfare by Parashurama. I have brought him to you now. You may take him to your capital.'

Although King Shantanu still suffered the pain of his separation from Ganga, he was overjoyed on meeting his accomplished son. Upon returning to his capital Hastinapur, he declared Devavrata to be the crown prince.

Devavrata grew up to be known as Bhishma. He was the grand-uncle of the Pandavas and the Kauravas.

Kunti's Boon, Birth of Pandavas

Kuntibhoja's foster daughter, Kunti grew up to be as intelligent as she was beautiful. She was always more interested in scriptures rather than the usual fun and games that girls of her age enjoyed. In those times, the brahmins and sages travelling through the capital would always pay a visit to the king. Kunti would love these visits and welcomed the learned men with much respect.

Once sage Durvasa visited Kuntibhoja. He stayed there for some time. Kunti was very happy. Durvasa was well-known for his short temper and cursing people. Everyone was scared to offend him, yet Kunti was not bothered. She looked after the sage like a devoted daughter.

Durvasa was impressed by the young teenager's faith, obedience and dedication to service, so much so, that he decided to bless her with a boon. It was in the form of teaching young Kunti a powerful mantra.

DID YOU KNOW?

Pritha and Vasudeva (Krishna's father) were children of Yadava chief, Shurasena. King Kuntibhoja was the son of Shurasena's sister. He was childless. Shurasena promised to give his first-born daughter to him. So, when Pritha was born, her father Shurasena gave her for adoption to Kuntibhoja, who renamed her Kunti.

'Whenever you invoke any god by chanting this mantra, he will visit you and bless you with a son.'

It was a powerful boon indeed, that is, if used wisely.

As most teenagers are, Kunti was curious. She decided to test the mantra. In the privacy of her room, she invoked Surya the sun-God. Lo and behold, Surya actually appeared!

'You called me Kunti, and I am here.' Surya smiled brilliantly.

'No, no! I was only trying to see if the mantra worked. Please go away!' Kunti pleaded.

'This is not a game, young girl! The mantra has to be respected. You have to bear the consequences of your deed.'

Soon, Kunti bore a son and was amazed to see the newborn already clad in a protective armour and earrings. Though it broke her heart to let go of the beautiful baby, she had to do it because she was not married.

KING PANDU

After King Shantanu's death, his son Chitrangada became king of Hastinapur. But he soon died in a battle and his younger brother Vichitravirya became the king. When Vichitravirya died, his elder son Dhritarashtra could not become the king because he was blind by birth. So the younger son Pandu was crowned king of Hastinapur.

Kunti placed the baby in a basket and set it afloat on river Ganga, praying for some kind-hearted person to find it and give a home to her son. This baby boy was saved and brought up by a charioteer and his wife like their own son. They named him Karna.

After some time Kunti married King Pandu of Hastinapur. In order to expand their kingdom further, the kings of those times married princesses of neighbouring kingdoms. So, Pandu also married princess Madri of Madra.

Pandu was a great warrior, ruled well, and expanded his kingdom considerably. Unfortunately, he could not have children due to sage Kindama's curse. What was it?

Once Pandu had gone for hunting and saw two deer. Without giving much thought, he shot at them. Imagine his shock, when just before dying, the deer turned into sage Kindama and his wife!

The angry sage cursed, 'As I am dying today, you will also die the moment you touch any of your wives!'

A heartbroken and remorseful Pandu renounced the kingdom and went to the forest with both his wives, Kunti and Madri.

While in the forest, they met some sages who told Pandu that without children there was no hope for him to ever go to heaven! That's when Kunti decided to tell him about her boon from sage Durvasa. As expected, Pandu was overjoyed.

Subsequently, Kunti used her boon to invoke Dharmaraja, god of justice, who blessed her with Yudhishthira. Then she invoked Vayu, god of wind, who blessed her with Bheema. Finally, Kunti invoked Indra, king of gods, and was blessed with Arjuna.

She then shared the mantra with Madri, who invoked the Ashvinikumars, the twin gods of healing, and was blessed with twins Nakula and Sahadeva.

The five boys grew up to be known as Pandu's sons, the Pandavas, who, after winning the Mahabharata war, ruled the land of Bharat Varsha. And it was made possible only because of sage Durvasa's boon to Kunti!

Meanwhile, Karna grew up as the charioteer's son. Because of his extraordinary archery skills, he was befriended by Duryodhana, the eldest Kaurava prince. Duryodhana gave Karna the respect he deserved by making him the king of Anga kingdom. From being labelled as a charioteer's son, Karna was now known as the king of Anga. It was natural for him to commit his allegiance to Duryodhana and the Kauravas.

Just before the war of Mahabharata, Kunti decided to meet Karna and tell him the truth about his birth. But it was too late!

Kunti hoped that her eldest son Karna would join the Pandavas in war. Though shocked by his birth-mother's revelation, Karna remained loyal to his mentor Duryodhana. He promised Kunti that he will not kill his Panadava brothers except Arjuna. And that, she will continue to be known as the mother of five sons.

This was a boon to the Pandavas, as Karna not only avoided attacking, but in fact spared his Pandava brothers. He tried killing Arjuna, but failed to do so, and died in the process. Kunti remained the mother of five sons.

At the end of the Mahabharata war, Yudhishthira was asked to perform the last rites of Karna, as a brother. The Pandava brothers were shocked when their mother Kunti told them the truth about Karna. They felt sad that Karna, the eldest of the Pandavas, was never given the respect he deserved. A royal prince by birth, he lived his life as a charioteer's son.

The worst part of all this was that they had committed the sin of killing their own brother! That's when, angry with his mother for keeping such a big secret from them, Yudhishthira cursed Kunti and the entire womankind that they shall never be able to keep secrets!

Karna, Born of a Boon but Accursed

Kunti's son from Surya, Karna, was found and adopted by Adhiratha and his wife Radha. Adhiratha was a charioteer at Kuru King Dhritarashtra's palace. The couple did not have any children, so they brought up Karna as their son, showering him with love and blessings.

Adhiratha gifted him a horse and wanted to teach him how to drive a chariot, but Karna was more interested in learning archery.

Dhritarashtra's sons—the Kauravas—and Pandu's sons—the Pandavas—were being trained in martial arts by Rajguru Drona. So, on Adhiratha's suggestion, Karna went to him to learn archery. Unfortunately, he was rejected outright!

'I only teach kshatriyas. You are a suta-putra. I cannot teach you!' Drona declared. Suta-putra means son of a charioteer, implying that Karna was of a lower caste.

A heartbroken Karna decided to approach Drona's teacher, the greatest martial arts teacher of all,

WHO WAS DRONA?

Drona was the teacher of Pandavas and Kauravas. He taught them military arts and the use of divine weapons. Once King Drupada insulted Drona, and the latter took revenge by sending his best student Arjuna to fight and defeat him. Subsequently, Drupada's son Drishtadyumna killed Drona in the war of Mahabharata to avenge his father.

Parashurama. But again, there was a catch. Parashurama taught only brahmins!

This time Karna did not want to lose the opportunity and wore the sacred thread of the brahmins when he approached Parashurama for lessons. It worked!

WHO WAS PARASHURAMA?

Parashurama was the sixth incarnation of Vishnu on Earth and is believed to be immortal.

Parashurama accepted him with delight. Karna turned out to be a sincere student, who learnt every martial art with diligence and dedication. Soon, he became an expert in whatever his teacher taught him.

Impressed with Karna's progress and his commitment, Parashurama taught him all that he knew. He declared Karna to be second to none in warfare! On the final day of his training in the forest, Parashurama felt tired and told Karna that he desired to lie down.

Karna immediately sat down so that Parashurama could put his head on his lap and rest.

Everything seemed to be going well for Karna thus far, but then the story takes a turn.

Parashurama had dozed off. Karna was happy. But Indra, the king of gods and father of Arjuna, was not happy with Karna's progress. He did not want Karna to be better than Arjuna!

Indra took the form of a blood-sucking insect and bit Karna on his thigh. It was a painful wound and it started bleeding. But Karna could not do anything without disturbing his guru's sleep.

Slowly, the blood trickled down to reach Parashurama's ear and he woke up. 'Whose blood is this?' he asked.

'Mine,' said Karna. Then Parashurama noticed the bleeding wound on Karna's thigh.

'You cannot be a brahmin! You would have screamed if you were. You must be a kshatriya to bear this kind of pain without wincing!' Parashurama was furious.

'Yes, I'm not a brahmin. But I'm not a kshatriya either. I'm a suta-putra. Please do not be angry with me!' Karna pleaded.

'You think you can come here wearing a false thread and deceive me into training you! I will curse you for this deceit! You will enjoy what I have taught you, but when you would need to use these skills, you will forget everything, and that will be your end!'

'Please don't do this! I had no intention of deceiving you. I'm not a kshatriya, so no teacher was willing to teach me. You were my only hope, as you taught non-kshatriyas.'

Parashurama's temper cooled down. He said, 'You shouldn't have lied. You could have discussed it with me. I cannot take back my curse, but I can assure you that people will always remember you as a great warrior.'

The curse did not seem so bad. But then, Karna had no idea about the war he would be fighting in future, where Parashurama's training would be needed!

One day, while practising archery in the forest, Karna shot an arrow blindly at an animal moving in the bushes. Assuming he had shot a deer, Karna went to the thicket. To his horror, he discovered that he had shot a cow!

Just then a brahmin came by. Looking at the dead cow, he started crying, 'You have killed my helpless cow! I curse you that you will be killed when you are helpless like her!'

For a warrior like Karna, this curse was devastating!

Once, when Karna was on his way home, he saw a girl crying. He asked her the reason. She told him that she was carrying clarified butter to her house, and it got spilt on the way.

Immediately, Karna offered a fresh bowl of clarified butter to her. However, she refused, saying that she wanted the same butter and not any other from anyone else.

Karna picked up the soil on which the clarified butter had fallen. He squeezed the soil so hard that the butter came out from it and filled the girl's bowl. While squeezing the soil, Karna heard a voice full of pain. It was the voice of goddess Earth.

She cursed Karna, 'You caused me pain to help the girl. Henceforth, when you will need my support the most, you will not get it!'

The three curses on Karna culminated on the battlefield of Kurukshetra, and became the cause of his end, a fatal blow to the Kaurava army.

It happened on the seventeenth day of the eighteen-day battle. Karna had turned upon Arjuna. The earth shook as these two extraordinary warriors fought. As the fight intensified, the force of Arjuna's arrows kept on pushing Karna's chariot back.

Karna had been keeping a weapon especially to be used against Arjuna. He used it now, but, just as it came near Arjuna's head, Krishna pressed the chariot down a little into the slushy ground. The weapon carried off Arjuna's crown, saving his head.

Disappointed at not being able to get the better of Arjuna, Karna tried to move his chariot forward, but one of its wheels got stuck in the mud, because of goddess Earth's curse. On top of it, Karna forgot the use of all the divine weapons that he had acquired from Parashurama as per his curse!

Karna got down from his chariot to free its wheel and asked Arjuna to give him some time. But Krishna reminded Arjuna of the way his own son Abhimanyu was killed by Karna stabbing him on the back. So, showing no mercy to Karna, Arjuna sliced off his head with an arrow. Karna died a helpless death, fulfilling the brahmin's curse.

ABOUT THE AUTHOR

SUNITA PANT BANSAL is a renowned mythologist, storyteller, and author with a career spanning over four decades. Throughout her journey, she has worn many hats, excelling as a writer, editor, publisher, and entrepreneur.

She has led publishing houses and founded as well as edited newspapers and magazines catering to readers in India, the US, and the UK. Her contributions to the world of literature extend across multiple platforms, working with prestigious organizations such as Walt Disney, Warner Bros., Pearson Education, The Times of India, Hindustan Times, and ABP Group.

In addition to her global collaborations, Sunita ran her own publishing house creating books for audiences worldwide and served as the president of the esteemed Institute of Indology, further cementing her influence in the literary world.

Sunita has authored over 30 books for adults and young readers, delving into the philosophy of mythology. She has also written innumerable children's books focused on folk literature and scriptures, which have been translated into multiple languages and sold across the globe. Her books explore and reinterpret the timeless tales of characters from the epics and foundational texts for modern readers. Her storytelling blends mythology with history, making ancient tales accessible in today's context.

Sunita's contributions to publishing and literature have earned her recognition, including the 2024 AALEKH Women Achievers Award.

Amongst Sunita's recent bestsellers are *Everyday Gita, The Return of Vikram and Betaal, Puranas: The Origin of Gods and Goddesses, Ramayan: The Journey of Ram, Mahabharat: The Rise and fall of Heroes, and My First Stories of Saint Kabir: His Life and Lessons.*

Website: www.sunitapantbansal.com
LinkedIn & Instagram: @sunitapantbansal
Twitter & Facebook: @sunitapb

EXPLORE OUR OTHER MYTHOLOGY TITLES